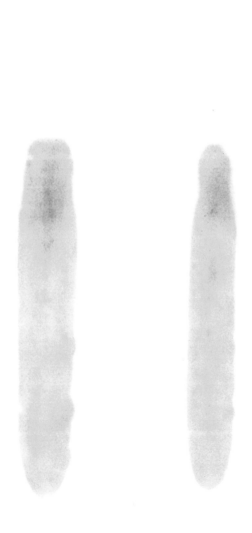

FILING RULES:
A Three-Way Divided Catalog.

BY

Grant W. Morse

Linnet Books
1971

© 1971 by The Shoe String Press, Inc.
Hamden, Connecticut 06514
ISBN: 0-208-01150-1
Library of Congress Catalog Card Number: 70-146702

First printing 1971
Second printing 1972
Third printing 1977

Contents

iii

Preface

The advantages of dividing a card catalog, index, or directories into the three basic divisions of information (author, title, and subject) are seen in the recent trend toward this practice by libraries. However, a comprehensive guide to filing in three divisions has not appeared. New rules are suggested; older ones no longer applicable to 3-way card catalogs are eliminated. The choice of rules and their application to card catalogs, indexes, and directories are to simplify a very complex tool for the user and to make filing a less cumbersome task. These rules make it possible to have all library card catalog filing accomplished by nonprofessional staff, enabling professional librarians to pursue professional work.

Although the Ala Rules for Filing Catalog Cards (2nd ed.) is comprehensive, the rules are often not compatible to a three-way divided catalog. Presented here is a new set of rules which meet more adequately the needs of a three-way divided card catalog, as well as the needs for indexes and compiling directories. Rules in general supplement tne A.L.A. rules for filing catalog cards. Nevertheless, similar rules are often stated somewhat differently.

Also, there is no attempt to create new types of headings. The form of headings chosen by the Anglo-American Cataloging Rules are not in question here. The chief concern here is to take the heading forms which exist in cataloging and adapt them to a three-way divided card catalog. The only concern with cataloging rules is when cross-references should be made, primarily those involving old and new forms in the Anglo-American Cataloging Rules.

The development of automated methods of filing will result in changes in the form of entries in library card and book catalogs. However, the rules in this book will remain basically the same because of its strict alphabetical arrangement, disregarding punctuation and form of headings. The choices of rules were with the view that both filer and user must benefit—the user always being preferred when possible. Therefore, few exceptions or alternative rules are given. It is believed that alternative rules may cause more confusion than aid for the reader. The Ala Rules for Filing Catalog Cards will supply sufficient choices for those who enjoy making decisions on most every rule.

v

Communication between the user and the information sought can best be maintained through the combination of the three-way divided catalog and a strict alphabetical arrangement.

I would like to thank the many librarians and friends who have contributed helpful suggestions for this guide to filing rules. Special thanks go to my library staff; Mr. Thomas Fitz, Mrs. Robert Hyllested, and Mrs. Bernard Uchytil who have contributed their professional knowledge, skills, and time in proofreading, in preparing this manuscript.

Rule I

Basic Rule

1. Arrange word by word. A "word" is an element which can stand alone as an utterance,
2. Alphabetize letter by letter to the end of each word in the order of the English alphabet, A through Z,
3. Arrange all modified and special letters as if they were unmodified:

CIGÜENA	as	CIGUENA
CAPUCHÓN	as	CAPUCHON
CRATÆGUS	as	CRATAEGUS
CRÊTE	as	CRETE
CǍPEK	as	CAPEK
ENCYCLOPÆDIA	as	ENCYCLOPAEDIA

For variant spelling see Rules II, point 7; IV; VI

4. Arrange line by line, beginning with the top line, to the end of the entry. Lengthy added headings requiring two or more lines for typing are treated as though they were all one continuous line for alphabetical purposes.

EXAMPLES OF RULE I*

AUTHOR	TITLE
Adair, Douglass	Engineers unlimited
Adams, Alexander B.	Engines and trains
Adams, Alexander John	England and the Near East
Adams, Andy	English historical documents
Adams, Elie	Englishe dogges
Adamson, Arthur	Englishman
Adamstone, Frank	Englishmen and others
Adler, Jacob	Enigma of drug addiction

SUBJECT

ARKANSAS

---

* The letter filed on is underlined.

ARKANSAS - HISTORY
ART
ART - ADDRESSES, ESSAYS, LECTURES
ART - CATALOGS
ART - EXHIBITIONS
ARTISTS
ARTISTS - DICTIONARIES AND ENCYCLOPEDIAS

Rule II

The Rule to Disregard

The purpose of punctuation is to clarify and make meaningful the entry heading, not for the purpose of alphabetizing.

1. Disregard all punctuation marks:
   (a) period (.)
   (b) dash (—)
   (c) colon (:)
   (d) parentheses [()]
   (e) apostrophe (') — see point 2 following this one
   (f) comma (,)
   (g) semicolon (;)
   (h) question mark (?)
   (i) brackets ([])
   (j) hyphen (-)—see point 7 below

Examples:

AUTHOR

Chicago. University. Law School
Michigan. University. Center for Research on Conflict
  Resolution
United Nations. Department of Public Information
United Nations. Statistical Office
Yale University. Studies in national policy, 4.

TITLE

Mozart handbook
Mozart: His character, his work
Mozart: the man and his work
Mozart's Librettos
Thoreau: A writer's Journal
Thoreau Handbook
Thoreau: Man of Concord

SUBJECT

EDUCATION
EDUCATION - ADDRESSES, ESSAYS, LECTURES
EDUCATION - AIMS AND OBJECTIVES
EDUCATION AND STATE
EDUCATION - BIBLIOGRAPHY
EDUCATION, ELEMENTARY
EDUCATION, HIGHER
EDUCATION - HISTORY
EDUCATION, SECONDARY
EDUCATION - SOUTH AFRICA
EDUCATIONAL ASSOCIATIONS

Note that all punctuation in subject card headings is disregarded.

2. Disregard apostrophe in words, both elided and posses-
    sive; arrange as they are printed (one word), and not as
    though spelled in full.

Examples:

AUTHOR SECTION

Obaid, Antonio
O'Ballance, Edgar
Obourn, Ellsworth
O'Brady, Frederic
O'Brian, John
O'Callaghass, Denis
Ocampo, Victoria
O'Casey, Sean
Ochsner, Alton
O'Connell, Ann
Odom, William
O'Donnell, Barry
Odum, Eugene

TITLE SECTION

Mannerism and habit
Man's best friend
Mansion in the sky
Who am I
Who was who...
Wholesale and retail trade...
Who'll mind Henry?

Who<u>m</u> God chooses
Who'<u>s</u> afraid?
Who's <u>W</u>ho
Who's who <u>i</u>n America
Whos<u>e</u> world

SUBJECT SECTION

D'ARUSMONT, FRANCES (WRIGHT), 1795-1852--FICTION
DA<u>T</u>E
D'A<u>V</u>ENANT, SIR WILLIAM, 1606-1668
DAV<u>I</u>D, KING OF ISRAEL

3. Disregard most signs and symbols, i.e., ???, ---,
    . . . , etc.

    The <u>b</u>lue pavilion
    ... <u>D</u>ebate index...
    "D<u>o</u>uble profit" in Macbeth
    The <u>F</u>ox from his lair
    ... And <u>s</u>hed a bitter tear

Exceptions: If the sign or symbol in a title is spoken as a
part of the title, it is to be regarded and filed as though it
were written out in the language of the title. Also applicable
to some subject headings. (See also Rule VI, point 1.)

"How to make $	Filed as:	How to make <u>dollars</u>
The + and − of gambling	" "	The <u>plus</u> and <u>minus</u> of gambling
Sam & Son Returns	" "	Sam <u>and</u> Son Returns
Ten % Chance to live	" "	Ten <u>percent</u> chance to live
2 + 2 = 3	" "	T wo <u>plus</u> <u>two</u> <u>equals</u> <u>three</u>

Other typical signs and symbols are ¢ (cents) and # (number).
If only nonalphabetic forms exist for an author or title and
they have no pertinent verbal equivalents, arrange them before the letter A. Disregard these forms following words
and file on the words:

        **
        ***
        _____
        _____?

A.
Adams, Andy
A.L.A.
Alexander, William

4. Disregard typography in filing, i.e., italics, etc. File italics the same as any other typography.
5. Disregard titles of honor and distinction such as Capt., Dr., Hon., Lady, Msgr., Sir, and so forth before an author's name and names used as subjects.

> Chambers, Sir Edmund Kerchever, 1866-
> (File as: Chambers, Edmund Kerchever, 1866-)

OR

> cross out the "Sir,"
> Chambers, ~~Sir~~ Edmund Kerchever, 1866-

6. Disregard initial articles in the nominative case in all languages but not within a title or subject.

Exceptions: (1) When the initial article contains a prepositional element, it is regarded; (2) as asterisk (*) preceding an article in the sample below indicates the same form is also used for the numeral "one" and therefore must be regarded in filing in all languages. If you are not certain whether it is an initial article or a numeral, assume it to be an article and disregard it. (See also, Rule III, point 2.)

French	English	German	Italian	Spanish
l'	a	der	il, lo	el, los
le	an	die	i, gl', gli	la, las
la	the	das	la, le	*un
les		*ein	l'	*una
*un		*eine	*un, *uno	
*une			*una, *un	

"A" is for Apple Pie (in this case the article "A" is used as a letter of the alphabet and is regarded in filing)
Advances in radio research
The advantages of dark
Advantages of the small local church
Adventure in liberty
The adventure into thought

An adventure with people
La aventura equivocial de Lope de
El concierto de San Ovidio
Les deux poemes de la folie tristan

7. Hyphenated words or names are arranged as one word.
The hyphen is disregarded. (See also Rule III, point 2.)

TITLE

Anticapitalistic mentality
Anti-Christianity of Kierkegaard
Anticoagulants and fibrinolycins
Anti-corn law league
Antifederalist papers
A handbook for modelling
A hand-book for travellers
A handbook of general knowledge
Handwork done by children
Hand-work methods
A handwriting manual
Handy man of the year
Handy man wanted
Handy-man of the year
Handy-man wanted

AUTHOR

Hall, Edward
Hall Williams, John
Halladay, Anne
Hallam, William
Hall-Edwards, Paul
Halliwell, Leslie
Halliwell-Philipps, James
Hallman, Victor
Hall-Quest, Olga
Halls, Giraldine
Saint Ambrose
Saint Vincent
Saint-Denis, Michael
Sainte-Deuve, C. A.
Saintine, X.B.
Saintsbury, George

Saint-Simon, Claude
Saint-Vallier, Jean
Sainz, Gustavo

SUBJECT

ANTIBIOTICS
ANTI-COAGULANTS
ANTIETAM, BATTLE OF, 1862
ANTI-NAZI MOVEMENT
ANTS
CHIEH, CHEN-KUO
CH'IEN-LUNG, EMPEROR OF CHINA
CHIGA (BANTU TRIBE)
SADDLERY
SAFE-DEPOSIT COMPANIES
SAFETY EDUCATION

8. Ignore dates following an author, except when distin-
guishing between two authors with the same name, the
earlier date being first.

Anderson, Hans Christian, 1805–1875
    Andersen's Fairy tales
Anderson, Hans Christian
    Emperor and the nightingale
Anderson, Hans Christian, 1805–1875
    Little Mermaid
Anderson, John, 1893-1962
Anderson, John, 1931-
Anderson, John S., 1789-1850
Anderson, Paul
Anderson, Paul M., 1907-
Anderson, Paul M., 1913-

9. Disregard all material showing relationship of a person to
a work such as, jt. author, tr., ed., comp., illus., and so
forth in filing. The designation "pseud." after a name should
be disregarded. In other words, if a person is editor, author, and translator of separate works, they are interfiled
as stated in Rule I.

Anderson, John, ed. Definition of God
Anderson, John, jt. author. Delectable past
Anderson, John. Vampire Cookbook
Anderson, John, ed. Volunteers for Peace

10. Disregard the initial articles and forms:

    al-, el-, ad-, ar-, az- prefixed to Arabic names.
    ha-, he- prefixed to Hebrew names.
    (See also under NAMES Rule III, point 1.)

Rule III

Names

This rule applies to all sections of the catalog.

1. Arrange a name with a prefix as one word, i.e., de, du, van, von. Initial articles, el, de, etc., are treated as a prefix when part of a name in all languages and are thus filed on. Cross-references may be made when thought useful. (See also Rule II, point 10, as an exception and Rule III, point 5.)

AUTHOR SECTION

    Dean, Howard E.
    De Angeli, Arthur C.
    Dearborn, Terry H.
    De Armand, David W.
    Dearmer, Percy
    De Barr, A. E.
    Debicki
    De Camp, Lyon S.
    Decarlo, V. J.
    Vanags, Alexander
    Van Arsdel, Wallace B.
    Vance, B. Bernarr
    Vandell, Robert F.
    Van de Luyster, Nelson
    Vanderbilt, Amy

TITLE SECTION

    Definition of Good
    De Gaulle and the world
    Delectable past
    De Lee's Obstetrics for Nurses
    De Lesseps: Builder of the Suez
    Delinquency and Child Guidance
    De Menil Collection
    Demetrios of Greece
    The El Capitan Peak

Elden Mountain story
The Elephant that went astray
El Paso, the City of Pleasure
Vampire Cookbook
Vancouver's Discovery of Puget Sound
Van Dean Manual
Van Goor's Concise Indonesian Dictionary
Van Nostrand Atlas of the World
Volunteers for Peace
Von Richthofen and the Flying Circus
Von Ryan's Express

SUBJECT SECTION

DEBATES AND DEBATING
DE BOW, JAMES
DEBTOR AND CREDITOR
DE HAVILLAND COMPANY
DELAWARE - HISTORY
VALLEY FORGE, PA.
VAN ALLEN RADIATION BELTS
VANBRUGH, SIR JOHN, 1664-1726
VAN BUREN, MARTIN, PRES. U.S., 1782-1862
VAN TIL, CORNELIUS, 1895
VAPOR PRESSURE

2. Compound names without a hyphen are filed as separate words. (See Rule II, point 7, for hyphenated names.)

AUTHOR SECTION

Saint Amand, J. E.
Saint, Dora
Saint John, Harold
Saint, Reginald
Saint Simon, Claude
Saint Vincent, Isobel
Saint-Aubyn, Giles
Saint-Denis, Michel
Sainte-Beuve, Augustine
Sainthill, London
Saintsbury, George
Saint-Simon, Henri
Saint-Vallier, Jean Baptiste
Saisselin, Rimy G.

TITLE SECTION

Saint among Savages
Saint Augustine on Personality
Saint in Hyde Park
Saint James in Spain
Saint Just: Apostle of the Terror
Saint Nicholas and the Tub
Saint of Ardent Desires
Saint Thomas and the Unconscious Mind
Sainte-Boune to Baudelaire
Sainte-John Perse
Saintmaker's Christmas Eve
Saints: Adventures in Courage
Saints and Scholars

SUBJECT SECTION

SAINT ANDREW ISLAND, COLOMBIA
SAINT LOUIS - HISTORY
SAINTE-BEUVE, CHARLES AUGUSTIN, 1804-1869
SAINT-EVREMOND CHARLES DE MARGUETEL DE
 SAINT-DENIS, SEIGNEUR DE, 1613-1703
SAINT-MARTIN, LOUIS CLAUDE DE, 1743-1803
SAINTS
SAINTS - ART
SAINTS - LEGENDS
SAINT-VICTOR, RENE MARIE EMILE VIVANT - FICTION
SAKKARA - ANTIQUITIES
 (See also Rule IV.)

3. Surnames, forenames, corporate, and place names

   Definitions:

   Forename — a name that precedes the family name or
   surname; a first name; a given name; not
   inherited.

   Surname — a family name; the name which a person
   has in common with other members of his
   family.

   Place name — a name of a geographical locality, i.e.,
   city or town.

Corporate name — a name of a society, institution, government department, bureau, or other organized body.

Proper name — a personal and geographical name.

Compound name — consists of two or more separate words.

(a) They are interfiled and arranged as stated in Rule I.
(b) The arrangement of names will be as follows:
   (1) Initials alone precede all surnames beginning with the same letters. Initials are treated as though they formed a word. (See Rule IV, point 3.)

   H.
   H. E.
   Henry
   Henry, C. W.
   H. W.

   (2) Surnames only or forename only

   Henry
   Henry, A. F.
   Henry, Carl

   (3) Surname and/or forename followed only by initials (the initials precede all first names, etc., beginning with the same letters). Initials are treated as though they formed a word. (See Rule IV, point 3.)

   Henry, Carl
   Henry, Charles
   Henry, C. W.
   Henry, George
   Henry, George A.
   Henry, George Andy
   Henry, G. W.

   (4) Surname followed by forename

   Henry, Carl
   Henry, Charles

   (5) Headings with dates, when used, (see Rule II, point 8), follow "like" initial headings, (in this case, surname, forename, etc.).

    Henry, Carl
    Henry, Carl, <u>1891</u>-1947
    Henry, Charles

(6) Roman numerals following names of kings, and so
forth are ignored in alphabetizing, except when they
are needed to distinguish between two like entries.
(See also Rule VI.)

    Henry, Charles
    Henry, David
    Henry VII, Earl of Richmond
    Henry, George
    Henry I, King of England
    Henry II, King of England
    Henry VIII, King of England
    Henry II, King of Scotland
    Henry, Paul
    Henry, Raspe

(7) Corporate entries (institutions, organizations,
societies, etc.), are to be arranged in the same
way as those for personal author headings <u>and</u>
interfiled.

    Henry, Charles
    Henry College, Campbell, Tex.
    Henry, David
    Henry, Father, 1881-1939
    Henry Ford Hospital Symposium
    Henry Ford Trade School, Dearborn, Mich.
    Henry, George

(8) Compound names are interfiled disregarding punctuation, as one word if hyphenated or as separate
words if not.

    Henry, Paul
    Henry Raspe
    Henry Raspe, David
    Henry, William
    Henry-Greard, O.
    Henry-Lacaze, Lydie
    Henryson, Robert

(9) Surnames followed only by appellative or designation are interfiled as in Rule I.

Henry, David
Henry, Duke of Lancaster, 1299?-1361
Henry, Earl
Henry VII, Earl of Richmond
Henry, Father, 1881-1939
Henry, George
Henry, Mr.
Henry, Paul
Henry, Professor
Henry, William

AUTHOR SECTION

(1) H.
(1) H. E.
(2) Henry
(3) Henry, A. F.
(4) Henry, Carl
(4 & 5) Henry, Carl, 1891-1947
(4) Henry, Charles
(7) Henry College, Campbell, Tex.
(3) Henry, C. W.
(4) Henry, Sir David   (See also Rule II, point 5.)
(3 & 4) Henry, David A.
(9) Henry, Duke of Lancaster, 1299?-1361
(7) Henry E. Huntington Library and Art Gallery
(6 & 9) Henry VII, Earl of Richmond
(4) Henry, Sir Edward Richard, bart., 1850-1931   (See
                           also Rule II, points 5 and 9.)
(9) Henry, Father, 1881-1939
(7) Henry Ford Hospital Symposium
(7) Henry Ford trade school, Dearborn, Mich.
(8 & 9) Henry Frederick, Duke of Cumberland, 1745-1790,
         defendant
(4) Henry, George, tr.
(3 & 4) Henry, George A.
(3 & 4) Henry, George Adams
(3) Henry, G. W.

(4) Henry, Mrs. Jennie (Dow), 1885-   (See also Rule II,
                                                        point 5.)
(6 & 9) Henry I, King of England
(6 & 9) Henry II, King of England
(6 & 9) Henry VIII, King of England, 1491-1547
(6 & 9) Henry II, King of Scotland
(6 & 9) Henry, VIII, King of the House of Tudor
    (9) Henry, Mr.
    (3) Henry, O.
    (3) Henry, O. B.
(3 & 5) Henry, O. D., 1921-
    (9) Henry of Avranches, 13th Cent.
    (9) Henry of Blois
    (9) Henry of Flanders
    (9) Henry of Huntingdon, 1084? -1155
    (9) Henry of Silegrave
    (4) Henry, Paul
    (9) Henry, Professor
    (8) Henry Raspe
    (8) Henry Raspe, David
    (7) Henry Street Settlement, New York
    (9) Henry the Black
    (9) Henry, the Minstrel, 15th cent.
    (9) Henry, the Minstrel, fl. 1470-1492
    (4) Henry, William
    (3) Henry, W. O.
    (8) Henry-Greard, O.
    (8) Henry-Lacaze, Lydie
    (4) Henryson, Robert
    (4) Henschel, Stan
    (1) H. W.

TITLE SECTION   (See Rule VI, point 1.)

    Henry Adams and Brooks Adams
    Henry Barnard on Education
    Henry Cabot Lodge: A biography
    Henry Purcell and the Restoration Theatre
    Henry Purcell, 1659-1695: essays on his music
        (Sixteen Fifty-nine to Sixteen Ninety-five: essays on...)
    Henry Purcell, Sixteen Fifty-nine to Sixteen Ninety-five:
        His life...
    Henry VIII, and his times
        (Henry the eighth, and his times)

Henry VIII, and Luther
 (Henry the eighth, and Luther)
Henry VIII, and the Reformation
 (Henry the eighth and the reformation)
Henry the Explorer
Henry V
 (Henry the fifth)
Henry V, and the Invasion of France
 (Henry the fifth, and the Invasion of France)
Henry IV
 (Henry the fourth)
Henry II, the Vanquished King
 (Henry the second the Vanquished King)
Henry, the smiling dog
Henry Watkins Allen of Louisiana
Henry's Lincoln
Her Majesty's Customs and Excise

SUBJECT SECTION

HEMPSTEAD, N. Y. - HISTORY
HENRY, ALEXANDER, 1739-1824
HENRY COUNTY, TENN.
HENRY E. HUNTINGTON LIBRARY
HENRY, SIR EDWARD RICHARD, BART., 1850-1931
HENRY FREDERICK, PRINCE OF WALES
HENRY, JOSEPH, 1797-1878
HENRY II, KING OF ENGLAND, 1133-1189
HENRY II, KING OF ENGLAND, 1133-1189 - DRAMA
HENRY III, KING OF ENGLAND, 1207-1272
HENRY V, KING OF ENGLAND - FICTION
HENRY, PATRICK, 1736-1799
HENRYSON, ROBERT, 1430-1506
HEREDITY

4. In heading of noblemen, popes, and sovereigns, disregard
   epithets such as "the Conqueror," "the Great," "the Bold,"
   "the German," etc., when they come between the name and
   the designation.

   Name   epithet   designation

   William I, the Conqueror, King of England, 1027?-1087
   William I, THE CONQUEROR, KING OF ENGLAND,
                                          1027?-1087

Epithets are not used in new-form headings and the above
would appear:

William I, King of England, 1027?-1087
WILLIAM I, KING OF ENGLAND, 1027?-1087

The old and new forms of headings may be interfiled. A
line through the epithet makes it easier to note the alphabetical arrangement.

William I, King of England, 1027?-1087
William I, ~~the Conqueror~~, King of England, 1027?-1087
William I, King of England, 1027?-1087

WILLIAM I, KING OF ENGLAND, 1027?-1087
WILLIAM I, ~~THE CONQUEROR~~, KING OF ENGLAND,
                                             1027?-1087
WILLIAM I, KING OF ENGLAND, 1027?-1087

5. Within a heading, treat each part of a compound proper name,
    including articles, prepositions, and conjunctions, as a sepa-
    rate word, with the exception of prefixes in III, point 1 and
    elisions.

    Martin, David
    Martin de Almagro
    Martin de la Escalero
    Martin, Deese
    Martin del Campe
    Martin, Delahay
    Martin Deslandes
    Martin du Gard
    Martin, Duke

Rule IV

Initials and Abbreviations

1. Arrange all initials and abbreviations, acronyms, call letters of broadcasting stations, and so forth, in their individual alphabetical places in the card catalog itself.

<u>AUTHOR SECTION</u>

A.
A. G.
Agar, H. D.
Agar, Herbert
Agar, H. F.
Arieti, Silvavo
A. R. I. N. C. Research Corporation
Aston, Melvin J.

<u>TITLE SECTION</u>

A, a Novel
A is for Apple
Aaron Burr
Abandon Ship
A B C of Music
Abdominal Operations
A. W. Tozer
Awake and Sing

<u>SUBJECT SECTION</u>

DAYTON, OHIO
DDT (INSECTICIDE)
DEAD SEA SCROLLS
FLYING SAUCERS
FM BROADCASTING

2. Arrange initials, the abbreviations "U. S." and "GT. BRIT.," and so forth, as they are not as if spelled in full.

AUTHOR SECTION

United States War Dept.
Unity school of Christianity
Urwin, Kathleen M.
U. S. SEE ALSO United States
U. S. Armed Forces
U. S. War Dept.
Usher, Esther
Vsborne, Richard

TITLE SECTION

Doctor Zhivago
Doctors as Men of Letters
Downtown U. S. A.
Dr. SEE ALSO Doctor
Dr. Albert Schweitzer, Medical Missionary
Dr. Spock talks with mothers
Dracula

SUBJECT SECTION

UNITED STATES STEEL CORPORATION
UNITED STEEL WORKERS OF AMERICA
UNIVERSITIES AND COLLEGES
URUGUAYAN LITERATURE
U. S. see also UNITED STATES
U. S. - AIR FORCE
U. S. - HISTORY
USAGES OF TRADE

Exception: If subject subdivisions are abbreviated in subject headings, arrange them as if written in full. These
should be typed in full on catalog cards. The following abbreviations have been used by the Library of Congress:

Antiq.	Antiquities
Bibl.	Bibliography
Bio-bibl.	Bio-bibliography
Biog.	Biography
Bound.	Boundaries
Comm.	Commerce
Descr.	Description
Descr. & trav.	Description and travel
Dict. & encyc.	Dictionaries and encyclopedias

Direct.	Directories
Disc. & explor.	Discovery and exploration
Econ. condit.	Economic conditions
Emig. & immig.	Emigration and immigration
For. rel.	Foreign relations
Geneal.	Genealogy
Hist.	History
Hist. & crit.	History and criticism
Indus.	Industries
Manuf.	Manufactures
Period.	Periodicals
Pol. & govt.	Politics and government
Sanit. affairs	Sanitary affairs
Soc. condit.	Social conditions
Soc. life & cust.	Social life and customs
Stat.	Statistics

3. Arrange initials, abbreviations, and so forth, as though they were a complete word (disregarding inversions, spaces, and punctuations), i.e., I. B. M. as IBM.

AUTHOR SECTION

A. R. A.   (Ara)
Arieti, Silvavo
A. R. I. N. C. Research Corporation   (ARINC Research...)
Ariosto, Lodovico
Arjona, A.
Arjona, A. K.   (Arjona, Ak)
Arjona, Alberta
Arjona, J. H.   (Arjona, Jh)
Arjona, John
Arjona, L. M. S.   (Arjona, Lms)

TITLE SECTION

Iowa Whittlings
I. P. A. Review   (Ipa Review)
Ipcress File

SUBJECT SECTION

URUGUAYAN LITERATURE
U. S. - AIR FORCE   (Us - AIR FORCE)
U. S. PEACE CORPS   (Us PEACE CORPS)
USE TAX

4. When only a one letter initial exists at the beginning of the author, title, or subject, it is arranged as though it were a one letter word and placed before words beginning with the same initial letter.

AUTHOR SECTION

M. Robert Gomberg Memorial Conference
Misyurkeyen, I. V.
Mitan, G. Theodore

TITLE SECTION

Ezra, Nehemiah
F. Scott Fitzgerald
Fayette County Cemetery Inscriptions
FBI in Peace and War
Feiffer's Album

SUBJECT SECTION

D DAY see ...
DADAISM
I CHING
IBANAG LANGUAGE
IBM
I. G. FARBEN TRIAL, NUREMBERG, 1947-1948
IGLOOS

5. "See also" references from and to initials or abbreviations and the written-out forms are required. (See Rule VI.)

AUTHOR SECTION

Misyurkeyen, I. V.
M. I. T. SEE Massachusetts Institute of Technology
Mitan, G. Theodore

TITLE SECTION

Mister SEE ALSO Mr.
Mister Fisherman
Mistral
Mistress SEE ALSO Mrs.
Mozart's Operas
Mr. SEE ALSO Mister
Mr. Roosevelt's Four Freedoms
Mrs. SEE ALSO Mistress

Mrs. Beeton's Family Cookery
Much Ado about Nothing

SUBJECT SECTION

UNITED STATES see also U. S.
UNITED STATES
UNIVERSITIES AND COLLEGES
U. S. see also UNITED STATES
U. S. AIR FORCE

6. The following abbreviations denoting royal privilege at the
   beginning of foreign academies, societies, and so forth should
   be disregarded in any European language except English, un-
   less the omission would reduce the name to a common word
   or phrase:

   I.   (Imperiale)
   K.   (Koniglich, Kongelige, Kungliga)
   K. K.   (Kaiserlich - Koniglich)
   R.   (Real, Reale, Regia)

   COMPREHENSIVE EXAMPLES OF RULE IV

AUTHOR SECTION

A.
A. G.
Agar, H. D.
Agar, Herbert
Agar, H. F.
AGARD
Arieti, Silvavo
A. R. I. N. C. Research Corporation
Ariosto, Lodovico
Astle, Melvin J.
ASTM-TAPPI Symposium on Petroleum Waxes
Aston, John G.
IBM Education Department
Igot, Yves
IGY Word Data Center
Isbele, Warren E.
Iscoe, Ira
ISCTR, 8th
ISCTR, 9th
M. Robert Gomberg Memorial Conference

Misyurkeyen, I. V.
M. I. T. SEE Massachusetts Institute of Technology
Mitan, G. Theodore
Sainsbury, Peter
Saint SEE ALSO St.
Saint Claire
Saint Paul, Mother
Saint Pierre, Michel de
Saint-Denis, Michel
Saint-Simon, Henri
Saisselin, Rimy G.
Scole, Leo
St. SEE ALSO Saint
St. Clair, Robert
St. Martin, Georges
St. Vincent, Edwin
Staack, Hagen
United Press International
United States SEE ALSO U. S.
United States Air Force
United States Army
United States. Army air forces, 4th fighter group.
United States War Dept.
Unity School of Christianity
Urwin, Kathleen M.
U. S. SEE ALSO United States
U. S. Armed Forces
U. S. Surgeon General, Advisory Committee
U. S. War Dept.
Vsborne,   Richard

TITLE SECTION

"A" and "B" Mandates
The A Company
A to Z SEE ALSO A-Z
A to Z
A Was a Leader
Aaron Burr
AAUN
ABA
A. B. C., Madrid
The ABC of Collecting
A. B. C. Programs

"A"-14
A. L. A.
Algebraic Curves
A. M.
A-Z
The Azores
The Aztec Temple
Dock brief and other plays
Doctor SEE ALSO Dr.
Doctor Alone Can't Cure You
Doctor Zhivago
Doctors as Men of Letters
Downtown U. S. A.
Dr. SEE ALSO Doctor
Dr. Albert Schweitzer, Medical Missionary
Dr. Spock Talks with Mothers
Dracula
Draft and the Vietnam War
Ezra, Nehemiah
F. Scott Fitzgerald
Fayette County Cemetery Inscriptions
FBI in Peace and War
Feiffer's Album
F-86 Sabre (as if spelled: F-eighty-six Sabre)
Idylls of Theokritos
IE Review
IEE News
IEEE Proceedings
IEEE Spectrum
IEEE Transactions
If the Shoe Fits
Iowa Whittlings
I. P. A. Review
Ipcress File
Mistakes in Geometric proofs
Mister SEE ALSO Mr.
Mister Andrews School
Mister Fisherman
Mistral
Mistress SEE ALSO Mrs.
Mistress Malapert
Mozart's Operas
Mr. SEE ALSO Mister

Mr. Roosevelt's Four Freedoms
Mr. Willowby's Christmas Tree
Mrs. SEE ALSO Mistress
Mrs. Beeton's Family Cookery
Much Ado about Nothing
O. Henry Almanac
O. Henry Stories
Oars, Sails, and Steam
OAS and the United Nations
Oodles of Noodles
007 James Bond   (as if spelled: 0 0 seven James Bond)
Open and Closed Mind

SUBJECT SECTION

BRYCE CANYON NATIONAL PARK
B-17 BOMBER   (spelled as if: B-Seventeen Bomber)
BUCCANEERS
D DAY see ...
DADAISM
DAYTON, OHIO - FLOOD, 1913
DDT (INSECTICIDE)
DEAD SEA SCROLLS
FLYING SAUCERS
FM BROADCASTING
I CHING
IBANAG LANGUAGE
IBM
IBM 650 (COMPUTER)
IBM 1401 (COMPUTER)
IBM 7090 (COMPUTER)
ICA, PERU - SOCIAL CONDITIONS
I. G. FARBEN TRIAL, NUREMBERG, 1947-1948
IGLOOS
ROTC see U. S. ARMY RESERVE OFFICER'S TRAINING CORPS
ROTH, LILLIAN, 1910-
UNEMPLOYED - U. S.
UNESCO see UNITED NATIONS EDUCATIONAL, SCIENTIFIC
                AND CULTURAL ORGANIZATION
UNFAIR LABOR PRACTICES
UNITED STATES see also U. S.
UNITED STATES
UNITED STATES AIR FORCE ACADEMY
UNITED STATES STEEL CORPORATION

UNITED STEEL WORKERS OF AMERICA
UNIVERSITIES AND COLLEGES
URUGUAYAN LITERATURE - HISTORY AND CRITICISM
U. S. see also UNITED STATES
U. S. - AIR FORCE
U. S. - BIOGRAPHY
U. S. - HISTORY
U. S. PEACE CORPS
U. S. PROVING GROUNDS, ABERDEEN MD.
U. S. WEATHER BUREAU
USE TAX see also SALES TAX
USIA see UNITED STATES INFORMATION AGENCY
USSISHKIN, MENAHEM MENDEL, 1863-1941
UTAH - ANTIQUITIES
U -2 INCIDENT, 1960   (spelled as if: U -two incident, 1960)
VOYAGES AND TRAVELS
V -2 ROCKET   (as if spelled: V -two rocket)

Rule V

Numerals (or The Numbers Game)

For the purpose of alphabetizing, there are two types of numbers: those in which the number is spelled out as spoken in the language of the title, and those arranged in a numerical sequence or chronological order. All Roman numerals are treated the same as Arabic.

1. Title headings

Numbers may be part of a title. In this case, all numbers are arranged as if they were spelled out as spoken in the language of the title.

(a) When verbalizing a compound number for filing purposes, omit "and" in alphabetizing, except for fractions. Four digit numbers are counted as "thousands," not hundreds (except for dates).

6¼	Six and one fourth
6½	Six and one half
150	One hundred fifty
125	One hundred twenty-five
1001	One thousand one
1234	One thousand two hundred thirty-four

(b) When verbalizing a date for filing purposes, omit "hundred" and "and" in alphabetizing, except the dates which begin each century.

300	Three hundred
301	Three 0 one
331	Three thirty-one
422	Four twenty-two
907	Nine 0 Seven
1000	One thousand
1800	Eighteen hundred
1900	Nineteen hundred
1901	Nineteen 0 one
1919	Nineteen nineteen

```
1942        Nineteen forty-two
2000        Two thousand
```

(c) When a question arises as to whether a set of numerals is a "date" or a " number, " assume it to be a date and make a cross reference from the "number" (not used) to the "date" used.

(d) Cross references must be made from all possible forms of verbalizing numerals to that which is used.

Double 0 Seven SEE 00 Seven
One hundred blackboard games
007   (00 Seven)
Twenty Prose Poems
Zero Zero Seven SEE 00 Seven

(e) Arrange numerals in foreign languages as if spelled out according to the usage of that particular language.

(f) For numerals following names in titles see comprehensive examples of titles under Rule III, point 3.

COMPREHENSIVE EXAMPLES OF NUMERALS IN TITLES

TITLE	FILED AS
DNA: At the Core of Life Itself	
D-99	D-Ninety-Nine
Double 0 Seven SEE 00 Seven	
The Feast of Fear	
F-86 Sabre	F-Eighty-six Sabre
First American	
I & II Thessalonians	First and Second Thessa- lonians
1st Nine Months of Life	First Nine Months of Life
First 125 Years	First One Hundred Twenty- five Years
40 + 1	Forty Plus One
Forty Poems and Stories	
France: 1814-1919	France: Eighteen fourteen - nineteen nineteen
France in the Nineteenth Century	
France in the 16th Century	France in the Sixteenth Century
French: 3100 Steps to Master Vocabulary	French: Three thousand One hundred Steps to Master Vocabulary

French Wars of Religion
Henry Cabot Lodge: a biography
Henry the Explorer
Henvy V   Henry the fifth
Henry IV   Henry the fourth
Henry, the smiling dog
1914 Diary   Nineteen Fourteen Diary
1919   Nineteen Nineteen
Nineteen Twenties
1/2 is Mine   One Half is Mine
One Hundred & One   One Hundred and One
One Hundred Blackboard Games
150 Brief Sermon Outlines   One Hundred Fifty Brief
                                               Sermon Outlines

101 Puzzles   One Hundred One Puzzles
1,000,000 Centuries   One Million Centuries
1800 Riddles   One Thousand Eight Hundred
                                               Riddles
1001 Answers to Questions   One Thousand One Answers
    About Trees   to Questions about Trees
One Thousand Questions and
    Answers
1234 Modern End-Game Studies   One Thousand Two Hundred
                                               Thirty-four Modern End-
                                               Game Studies

One Thousand Years on Mound Key
1, 2, 3 - Infinity   One, Two, Three - Infinity
One World
007   00 Seven
12½ Main Street   Twelve and One Half Main
                                               Street
12:30 From Croydon   Twelve Thirty From Croydon
Twentieth Century Russia
20th Century Stage Decoration   Twentieth Century Stage
                                               Decoration
XXth Century Young People   Twentieth Century Young
                                               People

Twentieth-Century Music
20th-Century Teenagers   Twentieth-Century Teenagers
20 Grand Short Stories   Twenty Grand Short Stories
20,000,000 Tons Under the Sea   Twenty Million Tons Under
                                               the Sea

Twenty Prose Poems
20,000 Leagues Under the Sea   Twenty Thousand Leagues
                                                         Under the Sea
Twenty Years at Hull-House
29 Stories   Twenty-Nine Stories
201 French Verbs   Two Hundred One French
                                                         Verbs

Zero Zero Seven SEE 00 Seven

2. Subject and Author Headings

    (a) All numerals BEGINNING a heading are spelled out as
spoken in the language of the subject or author.

AUTHOR   FILED AS

1st Research Corp.   First Research Corp.
First, Ruth
First, Wesley
Nineham, Dennis
9th International Botanical   Ninth International Botanical
  Congress   Congress
Seventh Regiment Veteran Club
79th Division Association   Seventy-ninth Division
                                                         Association

Seventy-second
20th Annual Conference on...   Twentieth Annual Conference
                                                         on...

Twentieth Century Fund
Twenty-one Club, New York SEE
  Jack and Charlies "21," New York
22d Bombardment Group (U. S.) SEE
  U. S. Army Air Force...twenty-second bombardment...

SUBJECT   FILED AS

FOUR PICTURE TEST
4-H CLUBS   FOUR-H CLUBS
FOURTEENTH CENTURY
3-D see MOVING-PICTURES   THREE-D see ...
  THREE-DIMENSIONAL
THREE-HANDED BRIDGE
3-M see MINNESOTA MINING   THREE-M see ...
  AND MANUFACTURING

(b) <u>All numerals (dates and numbers) WITHIN a heading are
IGNORED in alphabetizing, EXCEPT when they are needed
to distinguish between two like entries.</u> Numerals, when
used, are always filed on (arranged in a numerical sequence
or chronological order) before a further alphabetical subdivision.

<u>Examples:</u>

Henry, Paul	
Henry, Paul <u>1857</u>-	(to distinguish only)
Henry, Paul <u>1896</u>-	(chronological order)
Henry Paul <u>E</u>mile	(further alphabetical subdivision)
<u>U</u>. S. Army Air Forces	
U. S. Army Air Forces. <u>4th</u> Air Force	(to distinguish only)
U. S. Army Air Forces. <u>7th</u> Air Force	(numerical sequence)
U. S. Army Air Forces. <u>14th</u> Air Force	(numerical sequence)
U. S. Army Air Forces. <u>A</u>ir Service Command	(further alphabetical subdivision)

(1) <u>Dates or centuries</u> following a heading are arranged
chronologically behind the initial heading (in case of dates)
by the first date, or if the same first date, by the second
date, the earliest being first. Centuries are filed as years
and precede all other dates of that century. B. C. dates
run in reverse order (620 B. C. is earlier than 50 B. C.).
The word "century" is not filed on.

<u>Examples:</u>

Smith, Samuel
Smith, Samuel, <u>1584</u>? -1662?
Smith, Samuel, <u>1720</u>-1776
Smith, Samuel, <u>1836</u>-1906
Smith, Samuel, <u>1904</u>-
Smith, Samuel <u>A</u>bbott

U. S. CIVILIZATION	
U. S. CIVILIZATION - 18TH CENTURY	(as 1700-)
U. S. CIVILIZATION - 1720-1865	
U. S. CIVILIZATION - 19TH CENTURY	(as 1800-)

U. S. CIVILIZATION - 20TH CENTURY   (as 1900-)
U. S. CIVILIZATION - 1945-

(2) Numerals (I, II, 1st, 2d, 81st, etc.) when filed on in a
heading are arranged after dates, in like headings and before a further alphabetical subdivision. The word "session"
is not filed on.

Examples:

Charles, Alfred
Charles I, King of Great Britain   (alphabetical)
Charles II, King of Great Britain   (numerical sequence)
Charles, Robert   (further alphabetical
                                              subdivision)

U. S. Congress
U. S. 63rd Congress, 1913-1915   (to distinguish only)
U. S. 63rd Congress, 1st session, 1913   (after dates)
U. S. 63rd Congress, 2d session,   (numerical sequence)
    1913-1914
U. S. Congress. Aviation Policy Board   (further alphabetical
                                              subdivision)

Note that the "63d" is ignored (Rule V, 2, b).

(3) Dates indicated by: (TO 1700), (TO 1914), or TO 1900,
the "TO" is not filed on. This date must precede all further subdivisions of dates because the "TO" assumes a
beginning at the earliest time to the date mentioned.

Examples:

ENGLISH LITERATURE - EARLY MODERN (TO 1700)
U. S. - CIVILIZATION
U. S. - CIVILIZATION - TO 1783
U. S. - CIVILIZATION - 18TH CENTURY   (as 1700)
U. S. - CIVILIZATION - 20TH CENTURY   (as 1900)
U. S. - CIVILIZATION - 1945-
U. S. - HISTORY, MILITARY
U. S. - HISTORY, MILITARY - TO 1900
U. S. - HISTORY, MILITARY, 1720-1865

COMPREHENSIVE EXAMPLES OF NUMERALS IN

AUTHORS & SUBJECTS

AUTHORS

Charles, Alfred Chalmers
Charles V, duke of Lorraine, 1643-1690
Charles VI, king of France, 1368-1422
Charles VIII, king of France, 1470-1498
Charles IX, king of France, 1550-1574
Charles I, king of Great Britain, 1600-1649
Charles I, king of Great Britain, 1600-1649, defendant
Charles II, king of Great Britain, 1630-1685
Charles, Robert Henry, 1855-1931
Charles, Robert Henry, 1882-
Harvard University. American Defense, Harvard Groups
Harvard University. Class of 1898
Harvard University. Class of 1930
Harvard University. Class of 1946
Harvard University. Computation Laboratory
Henry, Paul
Henry, Paul 1857-
Henry, Paul 1896-
Henry, Paul Emile
Henry, Pierre 1903-
Henry, Pierre 1906-
Louis Bonaparte, king of Holland, 1778-1846
Louis, duke of Burgundy, dauphin of France
Louis II, emperor, king of Italy
Louis, Henry
Louis XI, king of France, 1423-1483
Louis XII, king of France, 1462-1515
Smith, Samuel
Smith, Samuel, 1584? -1662?
Smith, Samuel, 1720-1776
Smith, Samuel, 1836-1906
Smith, Samuel, 1904-
Smith, Samuel Abbott
U. S. Army
U. S. Army, A. E. F., 1917-1920. 1st Division
U. S. Army, A. E. F., 1917-1920. 2nd Division
U. S. Army Air Forces

U. S. Army Air Forces. 7th Air Force
U. S. Army Air Forces. 8th Air Force
U. S. Army Air Forces. 8th Air Force. 25th Bombardment
Group
U. S. Army Air Forces. 8th Air Force. 71st Bombardment
Group
U. S. Army Air Forces. 8th Air Force. 19th Fighter Wing
U. S. Army Air Forces. Air Service Command
U. S. Army Air Forces. 5th Bombardment Division
U. S. Army Air Forces. 3d Bombardment Group
U. S. Army Air Forces. 305th Bombardment Group
U. S. Army Air Forces. 303d Bombardment Group (Heavy)
U. S. Army Air Forces. 14th Bombardment Squadron
U. S. Army Air Forces. 9th Bombardment Wing
U. S. Army Air Forces. 3d Bombardment Wing (Heavy)
U. S. Army Air Forces. Flying Training Command
U. S. Army Air Forces. 80th Interceptor Control Squadron
U. S. Army Air Forces. Office of Flying Safety
U. S. Army. Alaskan Command
U. S. Army and Navy Munitions Board
U. S. Army. 184th Antiaircraft Artillery Battalion
U. S. Army. 387th Antiaircraft Artillery Battalion
U. S. Army. 50th Antiaircraft Artillery Brigade
U. S. Army. Army, Pacific
U. S. Army. 1st Cavalry
U. S. Army. 1st Cavalry (Colored)
U. S. Army. 1st Cavalry Division
U. S. Army. 1st Cavalry (Volunteer)
U. S. Army. 3d Cavalry
U. S. Army. Continental Army
U. S. Army. II Corps
U. S. Army. IV Corps
U. S. Army. Corps of Engineers
U. S. Army. 35th Division
U. S. Army. 44th Division
U. S. Army. Eighth Army
U. S. Army. First Army
U. S. Army Map Service
U. S. Congress
U. S. 1st Congress, 1789-1791
U. S. 1st Congress, 1789-1791. House
U. S. 1st Congress, 1789-1791. Senate
U. S. 1st Congress, 1st session, 1789

U. S. 1st Congress, 1st session, 1789. House
U. S. 1st Congress, 2d session, 1789. House
U. S. 1st-2d Congress, 1789-1793
U. S. 40th Congress, 1867-1869
U. S. 63d Congress, 1913-1915
U. S. 63d Congress, 1st session, 1913
U. S. 63d Congress, 2d session, 1913-1914
U. S. 85th Congress, 1st session, 1957
U. S. 85th Congress, 2d session, 1958
U. S. 85th Congress, 2d session, 1958. House
U. S. 85th Congress, 2d session, 1958. Senate
U. S. Congress. Aviation Policy Board
U. S. Congress. Conference Committees, 1919-1920
U. S. Congress. Conference Committees, 1956
U. S. Congress. Conference Committees, 1957
U. S. Congress. Conference Committees, 1962
U. S. Congress. House
U. S. Congress. Joint Economic Committee
U. S. Congress. Senate
U. S. Congress. Senate. Special Committee on Aging
U. S. Constitution
U. S. Court of Military Appeals
U. S. Courts

SUBJECTS

AMERICAN LITERATURE
AMERICAN LITERATURE - 19TH CENTURY see also
    AMERICAN LITERATURE - EARLY 19TH CENTURY
AMERICAN LITERATURE - 19TH CENTURY
AMERICAN LITERATURE - 20TH CENTURY
AMERICAN LITERATURE - BIBLIOGRAPHY
AMERICAN LITERATURE - COLONIAL PERIOD
AMERICAN LITERATURE - EARLY 19TH CENTURY see also
    AMERICAN LITERATURE - 19TH CENTURY
AMERICAN POETRY - HISTORY AND CRITICISM
AMERICAN POETRY - HISTORY AND CRITICISM - 19TH CENTURY
AMERICAN POETRY - HISTORY AND CRITICISM - 20TH CENTURY
BIBLE. N.T. CORINTHIANS - COMMENTARIES
BIBLE. N.T. 1 CORINTHIANS - COMMENTARIES
BIBLE. N.T. 2 CORINTHIANS - COMMENTARIES
BIBLE. N.T. I JOHN
BIBLE. N.T. II JOHN

BIBLE. N. T. III JOHN
CHARLES V, EMPEROR OF GERMANY
CHARLES I, KING OF GREAT BRITAIN, 1600-1649
CHARLES II, KING OF GREAT BRITAIN, 1630-1685
CHARLES II, KING OF GREAT BRITAIN, 1630-1685 - FICTION
LOUIS, JOE
LOUIS VII, LE JEUNE, KING OF FRANCE, 1119-1180
  (See Rule III, point 4, "Le jeune: is an epithet meaning "the
  young".)
LOUIS XII, KING OF FRANCE, 1462-1515
LOUIS XIII, KING OF FRANCE, 1602-1643
LOUIS XIV, KING OF FRANCE, 1638-1715
LOUIS XVI, KING OF FRANCE, 1754-1793
LOUIS, MORRIS
LOUIS XVII, OF FRANCE, 1785-1795 - JUVENILE LITERATURE
LOUIS PHILIPPE, KING OF FRANCE, 1773-1850
LOUISBURG, SIEGES, 1745-1758
U. S. CONGRESS
U. S. 1ST CONGRESS, 1789-1791
U. S. 1ST CONGRESS, 1789-1791 - SENATE
U. S. 63D CONGRESS, 1ST SESSION, 1913. HOUSE
U. S. 63D CONGRESS, 1ST SESSION, 1913. SENATE
U. S. 63D CONGRESS, 3D SESSION, 1914-1915
U. S. 86TH CONGRESS, 1ST SESSION, 1959
U. S. - HISTORY
U. S. - HISTORY 17TH CENTURY
U. S. - HISTORY - 18TH CENTURY
U. S. - HISTORY - 1783-1809
U. S. - HISTORY - 1783-1865
U. S. - HISTORY - 1783-1865 - FICTION
U. S. - HISTORY - 19TH CENTURY
U. S. - HISTORY - 1809-1817
U. S. - HISTORY - 1815-1861
U. S. - HISTORY - 1815-1861 - SOURCES
U. S. - HISTORY - 1865
U. S. - HISTORY - 1865-1898
U. S. - HISTORY - 1933-1945
U. S. - HISTORY - 1945-
U. S. - HISTORY - CIVIL WAR
U. S. - HISTORY - CIVIL WAR - NEGROES
U. S. - HISTORY, MILITARY
U. S. - HISTORY, MILITARY (TO 1700)
U. S. - HISTORY, MILITARY - TO 1900

U. S. - HISTORY, MILITARY, 1720-1865
U. S. - HISTORY, MILITARY, 1900-1953
U. S. - HISTORY - REVOLUTION
U. S. - HISTORY - WAR OF 1812
U. S. - HISTORY - WAR OF 1898
U. S. - HISTORY - WAR WITH MEXICO, 1845-1848
U. S. - HISTORY - WORLD WAR, 1939-1945 see WORLD WAR,
     1939-1945
WORLD MAPS
WORLD TEST
WORLD WAR, 1914-1918 see EUROPEAN WAR, 1914-1918
WORLD WAR, 1939-1945
WORLD WAR, 1939-1945 - BATTLE-FIELDS
WORLD WAR, 1939-1945 - FICTION
WORLD WAR, 1939-1945 - OCCUPIED TERRITORIES
WORLD WAR, 1939-1945 - TREATIES
WORLD WAR, 1939-1945 - UNDERGROUND MOVEMENTS
WORLD WAR I see EUROPEAN WAR, 1914-1918
WORLD WAR ONE see EUROPEAN WAR, 1914-1918
WORLD WAR II see WORLD WAR, 1939-1945
WORLD WAR TWO see WORLD WAR, 1939-1945
WORLD'S FAIRS see EXHIBITIONS
WORMS

Rule VI

Words and Names with Variant Spelling

1. Arrange words and names having more than one possible spelling as they are spelled.

2. "See also" references are required to and from both spellings.

3. Arrange misspelled words in titles and author's name as if spelled correctly. Make a "see" reference from the misspelled form to the correct form.

4. Arrange a name with a prefix as one word (See Rule III, point 1).

AUTHOR, TITLE, AND SUBJECT SECTIONS

Johannessen, Kare L.
Johannesson, Eric
Johannsen, Albert
Johannsen, Robert
Johansen, Donald
Johansson, Arne Semb
Johnsen, Russell
Johnson, Albert
Johnson, Winifred
Johnson-Marshall, P. E. A.
M' SEE ALSO Mac, Mc
Mabry, Marion
Mac SEE ALSO M', Mc
Mac Adams, Howard
Macalaster, Andrews
Mac Alpine, John
Macatee, J. Edward
Macaulay, Wallace
Mac Donald, Donald
Madden, Robert
Mayer, Allan
Mazur, Paul
Mc SEE ALSO M', Mac

Mc Adam, John
Mc Cormick, James
Mc Williams, Robert
Mead, Emerson
M'Lane, Charles
Mlotkowski, Casimir
M'Neile, A. H.
M'Nelly, Theodore
Moak, Helen

TITLE SECTION

Color SEE ALSO Colour
Color and design
Color television
Colorful world of Babar
Colossus and other poems
Colour SEE ALSO Color
Colour guide to clouds
Colour vision
Colours of clarity
Colt automatic pistols
Hand and machine woodwork
Hand book SEE ALSO Handbook
Hand Book for telescope making
A hand on my shoulder
Hand woodworking tools
Handbook SEE ALSO Hand book
Handbook for beginning debaters
Handcrafts simplified
Hand-work methods of ...
Handwork of surgery

Rule VII

Sacred Books and Anonymous Classics

1. All so-called "main entry" cards for these books are filed
   in the title section of the card catalog. The reason is that
   almost all users would look in the title or subject sections
   for Bible or other sacred books. The same is true with
   anonymous classics. There is no logic to placing them in
   the author section. For librarians only—make a "see" reference in the author catalog section from, Bible SEE Bible in Title or Subject sections.

2. Because the form of headings may vary in the order of the
   elements, interfile and indicate in some way key word to
   be filed on (underline or make arrow).

   Bible. English. 1876
   Bible. English. 1901. American Revised
   Bible. English. 1948. Authorized
   Bible. English. Authorized. 1957
   Bible. English. Selections. 1944. Authorized
   Bible. English. Authorized. Selections. 1952
   Bible. English. New English. 1961
   Bible. English. 1955. Revised Standard

3. An exception to the general Rule V, point 1, on dates in
   Bible title headings must be made. This is due to the pecu-
   liar inclusion of the year of imprint after the name of the
   Bible version. Therefore, when "main entry" headings
   (filed in the title catalog) include dates, the dates are to be
   ignored in alphabetizing, except when they are needed to
   distinguish between two like entries.

TITLE SECTION

The Bible and the Church
The Bible book by book
Bible. Danish. 1911
Bible. English. 1901. American Revised
Bible. English. 1948. Authorized
Bible. English. 1957. Authorized

Bible. English. 1961. New English
Bible. English. 1955. Revised standard
The Bible in Milton's epics
Bible. Italian. 1471
Bible. Latin. 1913
Bible legend books
Bible: Myth or reality?
Bible. N. T. Apocryphal books. Acts
Bible. N. T. Apocryphal books. English
Bible. N. T. English
Bible. N. T. Ephesians
Bible. N. T. I Corinthians
Bible. N. T. I John
Bible. N. T. I Peter
Bible. N. T. Galatians
Bible. N. T. Gospels
Bible. N. T. Gospels. English
Bible. N. T. Greek
Bible. N. T. Revelation
Bible. N. T. II Corinthians
Bible. N. T. II John
Bible. N. T. Spanish
Bible. N. T. III John
The Bible on the world
The Bible on vacation and election
The Bible or evolution
Bible. O. T. Amos
Bible. O. T. English
Bible. O. T. Esther
Bible. O. T. Exodus
Bible. O. T. I Chronicles
Bible. O. T. Greek. 1821
Bible. O. T. Greek. 1906
Bible. O. T. Pentateuch
Bible. O. T. Psalms
Bible. O. T. II Chronicles
Bible. O. T. Syriac
Bible. O. T. Zechariah
Bible personalities
Bible, religion, and the public schools
Biblical archaeology

SUBJECT SECTION

BIBLE AND SCIENCE
BIBLE - ANTIQUITIES
BIBLE AS LITERATURE
BIBLE - BIBLIOGRAPHY
BIBLE - BIOGRAPHY
BIBLE - DICTIONARIES
BIBLE - GEOGRAPHY - MAPS
BIBLE - HISTORY
BIBLE IN LITERATURE
BIBLE. N. T. - INTRODUCTIONS
BIBLE. N. T. ROMANS - COMMENTARIES
BIBLE. N. T. VERSIONS
BIBLE. O. T. GENESIS - COMMENTARIES
BIBLE. O. T. PSALMS - PROPHECIES
BIBLE. O. T. SONG OF SOLOMON - PICTORIAL ILLUSTRA-
    TIONS
BIBLE PLAYS
BIBLE SERMONS
BIBLE STORIES
BIBLE - STUDY
BIBLE - STUDY - OUTLINES, SYLLABI, ETC.
BIBLIOGRAPHY

Rule VIII

Cross - References

1. Consider only the heading on a cross-reference or explanatory note for purpose of alphabetizing.

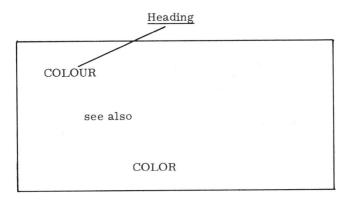

Heading

COLOUR

see also

COLOR

2. Combine all headings referred to alphabetically in one reference.

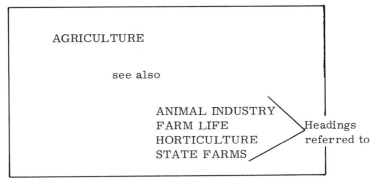

AGRICULTURE

see also

ANIMAL INDUSTRY
FARM LIFE
HORTICULTURE
STATE FARMS

Headings referred to

3. "See" references are filed on the heading not being used in their alphabetical places.

4. Cross-references should be made from possible forms to those used.

Heading not being used (possible form)

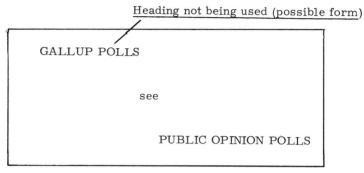

GALLUP POLLS

see

PUBLIC OPINION POLLS

5. "See also" references are arranged before entries of the same heading and are filed alphabetically by the words before the "see also. " These references refer to additional or related information.

M' SEE ALSO Mac, Mc
Mabry, Marion
Mac SEE ALSO M', M
Mac Adams, Howard
Mayer, Allan
Mc SEE ALSO M', Mac
McAdams, John
Mead, Emerson
USIA see UNITED STATES INFORMATION AGENCY
UTAH - ANTIQUITIES
WORLD WAR I see EUROPEAN WAR, 1914-1918
COLOUR see also COLOR
GALLUP POLLS see PUBLIC OPINION POLLS
HANDBOOK see also HAND BOOK
LABOUR see also LABOR
OIL see PETROLEUM

6. Filers must be on the alert for variations of spelling and form. Make appropriate references when needed.

Appendix I

Alphabetical Listings

As a further aid to learning and applying the previous rules, extensive alphabetical lists of subjects, authors, and titles are given in this appendix. The following suggestions are given with the intent of implementing the rules and these lists to your situation. Whether brief indexing is the aim or an extensive card catalog filing system is involved, applying these rules efficiently and effectively is desired.

Each rule has been interpreted and explained in light of its specific use, followed by brief sample alphabetical arrangements of headings. In this appendix these same rules and examples are related to a more representative general list approximating an actual index or library card catalog. Being familiar with these lists is an important step for the filer attempting to integrate the rules into actual filing.

Another step in the process of acquiring a working knowledge of these rules can be easily accomplished through practice cards. Type each of the headings from these lists on separate cards without the letters being underlined. Numbering the back of each practice card in their correct order makes for rapid checking of correct alphabetizing. Testing of potential filers with these practice cards becomes an efficient method of developing good filers. It would also be useful to have each practice card list a reference to the specific rule which applies to its location in the list. Misfiling could readily be corrected by the filer himself by referring to the proper rule immediately. This addition of the rules to the back side of the practice cards makes possible a very effective means of self-teaching of filing rules. It would be useful to add to this list of practice card headings in libraries having highly specialized subject collections.

Although each rule should be studied thoroughly, most brief indexes and directories can be compiled simply by referring to the lists of comprehensive examples. Bibliographical lists for research papers normally do not require knowledge of all rules—again the sample lists may suffice.

Note that in the three following lists the letter filed on is underlined. To avoid duplication, few names are given as samples in the
Subject list because the Author alphabetical list is also applicable to
subjects. A thorough familiarity with these lists will speed anyone's
ability to apply the rules in filing.

SUBJECTS

The letter filed on is underlined. The author alphabetical list is
also applicable to subjects.

ADAMS, JOHN, PRES. U. S., 1735-1826
AFRICA
AFRICA - HISTORY
AFRICA, SOUTH - RACE QUESTION
AFRICAN STUDIES
AGRICULTURE - BIOGRAPHY
AMERICAN LITERATURE
AMERICAN LITERATURE - 19TH CENTURY see also AMERICAN
    LITERATURE - EARLY 19TH CENTURY
AMERICAN LITERATURE - 19TH CENTURY
AMERICAN LITERATURE - 20TH CENTURY
AMERICAN LITERATURE - BIBLIOGRAPHY
AMERICAN LITERATURE - COLONIAL PERIOD
AMERICAN LITERATURE - EARLY 19TH CENTURY see also
    AMERICAN LITERATURE - 19TH CENTURY
AMERICAN POETRY - HISTORY AND CRITICISM
AMERICAN POETRY - HISTORY AND CRITICISM - 19TH CENTURY
AMERICAN POETRY - HISTORY AND CRITICISM - 20TH CENTURY
ANTHROPO-GEOGRAPHY - NORTH AMERICA
ANTHROPOLOGY
ANTHROPOLOGY - ABSTRACTS
ANTHROPOLOGY AS A PROFESSION
ANTHROPOLOGY, BIBLICAL see MAN (THEOLOGY)
ANTHROPOLOGY - METHODOLOGY
ANTHROPOLOGY, PREHISTORIC
ANTI-AIRCRAFT GUNS
ANTIBIOTICS
ANTI-COAGULANTS
ANTI-COMMUNIST MOVEMENTS - U. S.
ANTIETAM, BATTLE OF, 1862
ANTI-NAZI MOVEMENT
ANTIQUITIES

ANTS
ARKANSAS
ARKANSAS - HISTORY
ART
ART - ADDRESSES, ESSAYS, LECTURES
ART, ANCIENT
ART AND HISTORY
ART AS A PROFESSION
ART, BRITISH
ART CALENDARS
ART - CATALOGS
ART - EAST (FAR EAST) - HISTORY
ART - EXHIBITIONS
ART, IMMORAL
ART IN LITERATURE
ART INDUSTRIES AND TRADE
ART LIBRARIES
ART, MEDIEVAL
ART - PSYCHOLOGY
ART SCHOOLS
ART - STUDY AND TEACHING
ARTISTS
ARTISTS - DICTIONARIES AND ENCYCLOPEDIAS
BIBLE AND SCIENCE
BIBLS - ANTIQUITIES
BIBLE AS LITERATURE
BIBLE - BIBLIOGRAPHY
BIBLE - BIOGRAPHY
BIBLE COLLEGES
BIBLE - COMMENTARIES
BIBLE - DICTIONARIES
BIBLE. ENGLISH. 1951. AUTHORIZED
BIBLE. ENGLISH. 1951. REVISED STANDARD
BIBLE - GEOGRAPHY - MAPS
BIBLE - HISTORY
BIBLE IN LITERATURE
BIBLE. N. T. CORINTHIANS - COMMENTARIES
BIBLE. N. T. 1 CORINTHIANS - COMMENTARIES
BIBLE. N. T. 2 CORINTHIANS - COMMENTARIES
BIBLE. N. T. - INTRODUCTIONS
BIBLE. N. T. I JOHN
BIBLE. N. T. II JOHN

BIBLE. N. T. III JOHN
BIBLE. N. T. ROMANS - COMMENTARIES
BIBLE. N. T. VERSIONS
BIBLE. O. T. GENESIS - COMMENTARIES
BIBLE. O. T. - HISTORY
BIBLE. O. T. PSALMS - PROPHECIES
BIBLE. O. T. SONG OF SOLOMON - PICTORIAL ILLUSTRATIONS
BIBLE PLAYS
BIBLE SERMONS
BIBLE STORIES
BIBLE - STUDY
BIBLE - STUDY - OUTLINES, SYLLABI, ETC
BIBLE-CHRISTIAN CHURCH
BIBLIOGRAPHY
BOYCOTT
BOYS' CLUBS
BRYCE CANYON NATIONAL PARK
B-17 BOMBER   (B-SEVENTEEN . . .)
BUCCANEERS
CANADA
CANADA. ARMY. SEAFORTH HIGHLANDERS OF CANADA
CANADA GOOSE
CANADA - HISTORY
CANADA - HISTORY - TO 1763 (NEW FRANCE)
CANADA - HISTORY - 1763-
CANADA - HISTORY - 1763-1791
CANADA - HISTORY - 1763 - 1867
CANADA - HISTORY - 19TH CENTURY   (1800-)
CANADA - HISTORY - 1841-1867
CANADA - SURVEYS
CANADIAN ARCTIC EXPEDITION, 1913-1918
CHARITY
CHARITY ORGANIZATION
CHARITY-SCHOOLS
CHARLES V, EMPEROR OF GERMANY
CHARLES I, KING OF GREAT BRITAIN, 1600-1649
CHARLES II, KING OF GREAT BRITAIN, 1630-1685
CHARLES II, KING OF GREAT BRITAIN, 1630-1685 - FICTION
CHARLESTON (DANCE)
CHARLESTON, S. C.
CHIEH, CHEN-KUO
CHIGA (BANTU TRIBE)

CHINA (PEOPLE'S REPUBLIC OF CHINA, 1949-) - POLITICS
AND GOVERNMENT
CHRISTIANITY
CHRISTIANITY - 19TH CENTURY
CHRISTIANITY - 20TH CENTURY - ADDRESSES, ESSAYS, LEC-
TURES
CHRISTIANITY AND POLITICS
CHRISTIANITY - EVIDENCES
CHRISTIANITY IN LITERATURE
CHRISTIANITY - MIDDLE AGES
CLEMENS, SAMUEL LANGHORNE, 1835-1910
D DAY see WORLD WAR, 1939-1945 – CAMPAIGNS - NORMANDY
DADAISM
D'ARUSMONT, FRANCES (WRIGHT), 1795-1852 – FICTION
DATE
D'AVENANT, SIR WILLIAM, 1606-1668
DAVID, KING OF ISRAEL
DAYTON, OHIO
DDT (INSECTICIDE)
DEAD SEA SCROLLS
DEBATES AND DEBATING
DE BOW, JAMES
DEBTOR AND CREDITOR
DE HAVILLAND COMPANY
DELAWARE - HISTORY
DEOXYRIBONUCLEIC ACID
DEPARTMENT STORES
DIVORCE
DNA see DEOXYRIBONUCLEIC ACID
DRAMA - 20TH CENT. - HIST. &CRIT.
EDUCATION
EDUCATION - ADDRESSES, ESSAYS, LECTURES
EDUCATION - AIMS AND OBJECTIVES
EDUCATION AND STATE
EDUCATION - BIBLIOGRAPHY
EDUCATION, ELEMENTARY
EDUCATION, HIGHER
EDUCATION - HISTORY
EDUCATION OF CHILDREN
EDUCATION, SECONDARY
EDUCATION - SOUTH AFRICA
EDUCATIONAL ASSOCIATIONS
ENGLISH LITERATURE

ENGLISH LITERATURE - 18TH CENTURY
ENGLISH LITERATURE - 18TH CENTURY - HISTORY AND CRITICISM
ENGLISH LITERATURE - 19TH CENTURY
ENGLISH LITERATURE - 19TH CENTURY - HISTORY AND CRITICISM
ENGLISH LITERATURE - 20TH CENTURY - HISTORY AND CRITICISM
ENGLISH LITERATURE - DICTIONARIES
ENGLISH LITERATURE - EARLY MODERN (TO 1700)
ENGLISH LITERATURE - EARLY MODERN (TO 1700) - BIBLIO-
   GRAPHY
ENGLISH LITERATURE - EARLY MODERN (TO 1700) - HISTORY
   AND CRITICISM
ENGLISH LITERATURE - STUDY AND TEACHING
ENGLISH POETRY
ENGLISH POETRY - 18TH CENTURY
ENGLISH POETRY - 19TH CENTURY
ENGLISH POETRY - 20TH CENTURY - HISTORY AND CRITICISM
ENGLISH POETRY - ADDRESSES, ESSAYS, LECTURES
ENGLISH POETRY (COLLECTIONS)
ENGLISH POETRY - HISTORY AND CRITICISM
ENGLISH POETRY - INDEXES
ENGLISH POETRY - MIDDLE ENGLISH (1100-1500)
FLYING SAUCERS
FM BROADCASTING
FRENCH POETRY
FRENCH POETRY - 16TH CENTURY
FRENCH POETRY - 20TH CENTURY
FRENCH POETRY (COLLECTIONS)
GREAT BRITAIN see also GT. BRIT.
GREAT BRITAIN
GREAT LAKES
GREAT POWERS
GREECE
GROWTH
GT. BRIT. see also GREAT BRITAIN
GT. BRIT. - BIOGRAPHY - DICTIONARIES
GT. BRIT. - COLONIES - AMERICA
GT. BRIT. - EMIGRATION AND IMMIGRATION - HISTORY
GT. BRIT. - HISTORY
GT. BRIT. - HISTORY - TO 1485 B. C.
GT. BRIT. - HISTORY - TO 449 B. C.
GT. BRIT. - HISTORY - TO 55 B. C.
GT. BRIT. - HISTORY - 1066-1687
GT. BRIT. - HISTORY - 13TH CENTURY   (as 1200)

GT. BRIT. - HISTORY - 14TH CENTURY   (as 1300)
GT. BRIT. - HISTORY - 1689-1714
GT. BRIT. - HISTORY - 1760-1789
GT. BRIT. - HISTORY - 20TH CENTURY   (as 1900)
GT. BRIT. - HISTORY - ANGLO-SAXON PERIOD, 449-1066
GT. BRIT. - HISTORY - CIVIL WAR, 1642-1649
GT. BRIT. - HISTORY - ELIZABETH, 1558-1603 - FICTION
GT. BRIT. - HISTORY - GEORGE II, 1727-1760
GT. BRIT. - HISTORY - NORMAN PERIOD, 1066-1154 see also
    GT. BRIT. - HISTORY - 1066-1687
GT. BRIT. - HISTORY - NORMAN PERIOD, 1066-1154
GT. BRIT. - HISTORY - STUARTS, 1603-1714 - SOURCES
GT. BRIT. - POLITICS AND GOVERNMENT - 19TH CENTURY
    (as 1800)
GT. BRIT. - POLITICS AND GOVERNMENT - 1830-1837
GT. BRIT. - SOCIAL CONDITIONS
GT. BRIT. - SOCIAL LIFE AND CUSTOMS
GUANA INDIANS
GUILT
HEMPSTEAD, N. Y. - HISTORY
HENRY, ALEXANDER, 1739-1824
HENRY COUNTY, TENN.
HENRY E. HUNTINGTON LIBRARY
HENRY, SIR EDWARD RICHARD, BART., 1850-1931
HENRY FREDERICK, PRINCE OF WALES
HENRY, JOSEPH, 1797-1878
HENRY II, KING OF ENGLAND, 1133-1189
HENRY II, KING OF ENGLAND, 1133-1189 - DRAMA
HENRY III, KING OF ENGLAND, 1207-1272
HENRY V, KING OF ENGLAND - FICTION
HENRY, PATRICK, 1736-1799
HENRYSON, ROBERT, 1430-1506
HEREDITY
I CHING
IBANAG LANGUAGE
IBM
IBM 650 (COMPUTER)
IBM 1401 (COMPUTER)
IBM 7090 (COMPUTER)
ICA, PERU - SOCIAL CONDITIONS
I. G. FARBEN TRIAL, NUREMBERG, 1947-1948
IGLOOS

LOUIS, JOE
LOUIS VII, LE JEUNE, KING OF FRANCE, 1119-1180
LOUIS XII, KING OF FRANCE, 1462-1515
LOUIS XIII, KING OF FRANCE, 1602-1643
LOUIS XIV, KING OF FRANCE, 1638-1715
LOUIS XVI, KING OF FRANCE, 1754-1793
LOUIS, MORRIS
LOUIS XVII, OF FRANCE, 1785-1795 - JUVENILE LITERATURE
LOUIS PHILIPPE, KING OF FRANCE, 1773-1850
LOUISBURG, SIEGES, 1745, 1758
MAINE
MAKE-UP, THEATRICAL
MARK TWAIN see CLEMENS, SAMUEL LANGHORNE
MUNICIPAL GOVERNMENT - U. S. - CASE STUDIES
MUNICIPAL GOVERNMENT - YEARBOOKS
MUNICIPAL GOVERNMENTS - U. S.
MUSIC, POPULAR (SONGS, ETC.) - DICTIONARIES
NAMES, PERSONAL - U. S.
NAMES - U. S.
NEGROES - ADDRESSES, ESSAYS, LECTURES
NEGROES - BIBLIOGRAPHY
NEGROES - FLORIDA
NEGROES - HISTORY - SOURCES
NEGROES - NEW YORK (CITY)
NEGROES - POLITICS AND SUFFRAGE
NEGROES - SEGREGATION
NEW ENGLAND
NEW YEAR
NEW YORK. BASEBALL CLUB (AMERICAN LEAGUE)
NEW YORK (BATTLESHIP)
NEW YORK (CITY)
NEW YORK (CITY) - AMUSEMENTS
NEW YORK (CITY) - BIOGRAPHY
NEW YORK (COLONY)
NEW YORK (COLONY) - COMMERCE
NEW YORK. PUBLIC LIBRARY
NEW YORK (STATE)
NEW YORK (STATE) - HISTORY
NEW YORK (STATE) - HISTORY - CIVIL WAR
NEW YORK (STATE) - HISTORY - COLONIAL PERIOD
NEW YORK (STATE) - HISTORY - REVOLUTION
NEW YORK (STATE) - POLITICS AND GOVERNMENT - 1865-1950
NEW YORK TIMES. (INDEXES)

NEW ZEALAND
NEWARK
NEWBERY MEDAL BOOKS
ROME
ROME - ANTIQUITIES
ROME (CITY)
ROME (CITY) - HISTORY - TO 476
ROME - CIVILIZATION
ROME - HISTORY
ROME - HISTORY - ABORIGINAL AND EARLY PERIOD
ROME - HISTORY - CIVIL WAR, 49-48 B. C.
ROME - HISTORY - EMPIRE, 30 B. C. -284 A. D.
ROME - HISTORY - EMPIRE, 30 B. C. -476 A. D.
ROME - HISTORY - KINGS, 753-510 B. C.
ROME - HISTORY - REPUBLIC, 510-265 B. C.
ROME - HISTORY - REPUBLIC, 510-30 B. C.
ROME - HISTORY - REPUBLIC, 265-30 B. C.
ROME - HISTORY - TIBERIUS, 14-37
ROME - OFFICIALS AND EMPLOYEES
ROME - POLITICS AND GOVERNMENT
ROME - SOCIAL LIFE AND CUSTOMS
ROTC see U. S. ARMY RESERVE OFFICER'S TRAINING CORPS
ROTH, LILLIAN, 1910-
RUSSIA
RUSSIAN LITERATURE
RUSSO-JAPANESE WAR, 1904-1905
RUSSO-TURKISH WAR, 1828-1829
SADDLERY
SAFE-DEPOSIT COMPANIES
SAFETY EDUCATION
SAINT ANDREW ISLAND, COLOMBIA
SAINT LOUIS - HISTORY
SAINTE-BEUVE, CHARLES AUGUSTIN, 1804-1869
SAINT-EVREMOND CHARLES DE MARGUETEL DE SAINT - DENIS,
    SEIGNEUR DE, 1613-1703
SAINT-MARTIN, LOUIS CLAUDE DE, 1743-1803
SAINTS
SAINTS - ART
SAINTS - LEGENDS
SAINT-VICTOR, RENE MARIE EMILE VIVANT - FICTION
SAKKARA - ANTIQUITIES
SHAKESPEARE, WILLIAM - CONCORDANCES
SHAKESPEARE, WILLIAM - CRITICISM AND INTERPRETATION

SHAKESPEARE, WILLIAM, <u>1564</u>-1616 - CRITICISM AND INTER-
  PRETATION
SHAKESPEARE, WILLIAM, 1564-1616. <u>P</u>ARAPHRASES, TABLES,
  ETC.
SHAKESPEARE, WILLIAM - <u>S</u>OCIETIES, PERIODICALS, ETC.
SHAKESPEARE, WILLIAM - <u>ST</u>AGE HISTORY
SM<u>I</u>THSONIAN INSTITUTION
SM<u>O</u>CK-ALLEY THEATER
SMOCK<u>I</u>NG
SO<u>U</u>ND
SO<u>U</u>ND <u>P</u>RESSURE
SOUND-<u>W</u>AVES
ST<u>E</u>AM-ENGINES
ST<u>R</u>EET TRAFFIC
ST<u>R</u>EET-<u>R</u>AILROADS
STREET<u>S</u>
S<u>U</u>RF-B<u>O</u>ATS see LIFE-BOATS
<u>T</u>EACHERS - CERTIFICATION - U. S.
TEACHERS, <u>T</u>RAINING OF - U. S.
T<u>R</u>IALS (TREASON) - GT. BRIT.
TW<u>A</u>IN, MARK see CLEMENS, SAMUEL LANGHORNE
U<u>L</u>TRASONICS
ULTRA-<u>V</u>IOLET RAYS
UL<u>Y</u>SSES
U<u>N</u>EMPLOYED - U. S.
UNE<u>S</u>CO see UNITED NATIONS EDUCATIONAL, SCIENTIFIC AND
  CULTURAL ORGANIZATION
UNF<u>A</u>IR LABOR PRACTICES
UN<u>IT</u>ED STATES see also U. S.   (U. S. is filed as "Us")
UN<u>IT</u>ED STATES
UN<u>IT</u>ED STATES <u>A</u>IR FORCE ACADEMY
UNITED STATES <u>S</u>TEEL CORPORATION
UNITED ST<u>E</u>EL WORKERS OF AMERICA
UNI<u>V</u>ERSI<u>T</u>IES AND COLLEGES
U<u>R</u>UGUAYAN LITERATURE
URUGUAYAN LITERATURE - <u>H</u>ISTORY AND CRITICISM
U. <u>S</u>. see also UNITED STATES
U. S. - <u>A</u>IR FORCE
U. S. - <u>B</u>IOGRAPHY
U. S. - <u>C</u>IVILIZATION
U. S. - <u>C</u>IVILIZATION - <u>TO 1783</u>
U. S. CIVILIZATION - <u>1783</u>-1865
U. S. - CIVILIZATION - <u>1865</u>-1918

U. S. - CIVILIZATION - 20TH CENTURY   (as 1900)
U. S. - CIVILIZATION - 1945-
U. S. - CONGRESS
U. S. 1ST CONGRESS, 1789-1791 - SENATE
U. S. 63D CONGRESS, 1ST SESSION, 1913. HOUSE
U. S. 63D CONGRESS, 1ST SESSION, 1913. SENATE
U. S. 63D CONGRESS, 3D SESSION, 1914-1915
U. S. 86TH CONGRESS, 1ST SESSION, 1959
U. S. CONGRESS. SENATE - RULES AND PRACTICE
U. S. CONSTITUTION. 1ST-10TH AMENDMENTS
U. S. - CONSTITUTIONAL LAW - CASES
U. S. - CONSTITUTIONAL LAW - COMPENDS
U. S. - FOREIGN RELATIONS - 20TH CENTURY
U. S. - HISTORY
U. S. - HISTORY - 17TH CENTURY   (as 1600-)
U. S. - HISTORY - 18TH CENTURY   (as 1700-)
U. S. - HISTORY - 1783-1809
U. S. - HISTORY - 1783-1865
U. S. - HISTORY - 1783-1865 - FICTION
U. S. - HISTORY - 19TH CENTURY   (as 1800-)
U. S. - HISTORY - 1809-1817
U. S. - HISTORY - 1815-1861
U. S. - HISTORY - 1815-1861 - SOURCES
U. S. - HISTORY - 1865
U. S. - HISTORY - 1865-1898
U. S. - HISTORY - 20TH CENTURY   (as 1900-)
U. S. - HISTORY - 1933-1945
U. S. - HISTORY - 1945-
U. S. - HISTORY - CIVIL WAR
U. S. - HISTORY - CIVIL WAR - BIOGRAPHY
U. S. - HISTORY - CIVIL WAR - CAMPAIGNS AND BATTLES
U. S. - HISTORY - CIVIL WAR - NEGROES
U. S. - HISTORY - COLONIAL PERIOD - POETRY
U. S. - HISTORY - CONFEDERATION, 1783-1789
U. S. - HISTORY - CONSTITUTIONAL PERIOD
U. S. - HISTORY, MILITARY
U. S. - HISTORY, MILITARY (TO 1700)
U. S. - HISTORY, MILITARY - TO 1900
U. S. - HISTORY, MILITARY, 1720-1865
U. S. - HISTORY, MILITARY, 1900-1953
U. S. - HISTORY - PERIODICALS
U. S. - HISTORY - REVOLUTION
U. S. - HISTORY - REVOLUTION - CAUSES

U. S. - HISTORY - REVOLUTION - DICTIONARIES
U. S. - HISTORY - REVOLUTION - FRENCH PARTICIPATION
U. S. - HISTORY - REVOLUTION - REGIMENTAL HISTORIES -
   AMERICAN LOYALIST
U. S. - HISTORY - WAR OF 1812
U. S. - HISTORY - WAR OF 1898
U. S. - HISTORY - WAR WITH MEXICO, 1845-1848
U. S. - HISTORY - WORLD WAR, 1939-1945 see WORLD WAR,
   1939-1945
U. S. - IMPRINTS
U. S. PEACE CORPS
U. S. PROVING GROUNDS, ABERDEEN MD.
U. S. - RACE QUESTION - ADDRESSES, ESSAYS, LECTURES
U. S. - RELATIONS (GENERAL) WITH FOREIGN COUNTRIES
U. S. SUPREME COURT
U. S. WEATHER BUREAU
USAGES OF TRADE
USE TAX
USIA see UNITED STATES INFORMATION AGENCY
USSISHKIN, MENAHEM MENDEL, 1863-1941
UTAH - ANTIQUITIES
U-2 INCIDENT, 1960   (U-TWO ...)
VALLEY FORGE, PA.
VAN ALLEN RADIATION BELTS
VANBRUGH, SIR JOHN, 1664-1726
VAN BUREN, MARTIN, PRES. U. S., 1782-1862
VAN TIL, CORNELIUS, 1895
VAPOR PRESSURE
VAPOR-LIQUID EQUILIBRIUM
VAULTING
VAULTING - HORSE
VAULTS
VOYAGES AND TRAVELS
V-2 ROCKET   (V-TWO ...)
WAR AND RELIGION
WAR, ARTICLES OF see MILITARY LAW
WAR, COST OF
WAR, DECLARATION OF
WAR - ECONOMIC ASPECTS
WAR (INTERNATIONAL LAW)
WAR, MARITIME (INTERNATIONAL LAW)
WAR-SHIPS
WASHINGTON COUNTY, OHIO

WASHINGTON, D. C. WHITE HOUSE
WASHINGTON, MOUNT
WASHINGTON (STATE) - DESCRIPTION AND TRAVEL
WATER
WATER CHESTNUT
WATER CONSUMPTION
WATER, DISTILLED
WATER DISTRICTS
WATER GARDENS
WATER HEATERS
WATER METABOLISM
WATER - POLLUTION - ADDRESSES, ESSAYS, LECTURES
WATER, UNDERGROUND
WATER - UTILIZATION
WATER-BEETLES
WATER-BIRDS
WATER-CLOSETS
WATER-COLOR PAINTING
WATER-COLOR PAINTING - TECHNIQUE
WATER-COLORS
WATER-CRESS
WATER-GAS
WATER-JET
WATER-LILIES
WATER-MARKS
WATER-SUPPLY - SWEDEN - CONGRESSES
WATER-SUPPLY - U. S.
WORLD MAPS
WORLD POLITICS
WORLD TEST
WORLD WAR I see EUROPEAN WAR, 1914-1918
WORLD WAR II see WORLD WAR, 1939-1945
WORLD WAR, 1914-1918 see EUROPEAN WAR, 1914-1918
WORLD WAR, 1939-1945
WORLD WAR, 1939-1945 - BATTLE-FIELDS
WORLD WAR, 1939-1945 - FICTION
WORLD WAR, 1939-1945 - OCCUPIED TERRITORIES
WORLD WAR, 1939-1945 - TREATIES
WORLD WAR, 1939-1945 - UNDERGROUND MOVEMENTS
WORLD WAR ONE see EUROPEAN WAR, 1914-1918
WORLD WAR TWO see WORLD WAR, 1939-1945
WORLD'S FAIRS see EXHIBITIONS
WORMS

AUTHOR SECTION

**
***

_____?
A.
Abbott, Fred
'Abd Allah Sfer, pasha
'Abd al-latif
Abdullah, Achmed
Academy of Political Science
Adair, Douglass
Adams, Alexander B.
Adams, Alexander John
Adams, Andy
Adams, Edie
Adamson, Arthur
Adamstone, Frank
Adler, Jacob
Afanaser, Alexei
Afee, T.
Af Klintberg, Bengt
Afnan, Ruhi
A. G.
Agar, H. D.
Agar, Herbert
Agar, H. F.
AGARD
A Kempis, Thomas
Al, Eugene
Al, William
Al Akl, F. M.
A'Lapide, Cornelius
Al-Arron Family Group
Al-Bitruji
Albrecht-Carrié, René
Alexander, William
Al-Fasi, Alal
Alföldi, András
A Liu Kuang-Ching
Al-Marayati, Abid
Al-Shafti, Muhammad

Andersen, Hans Christian, 1805-1875. Andersen's fairy tales
Andersen, Hans Christian. Emperor and the nightingale
Andersen, Hans Christian, 1805-1875. Little mermaid
Andersen, John, 1893-1962
Andersen, John, 1931-
Andersen, Paul
Andersen, Paul J.
Andersen, Paul M., 1907-
Andersen, Paul M., 1913
Apanasevich, P. A.
Apel, Will
Aptheker, Herbert
Ap-Thomas, D. R.
A. R. A.
Arieti, Silvano
A. R. I. N. C. Research Corporation
Ariosto, Lodovica
Arjona, A.
Arjona, A. K.
Arjona, Alberta
Arjona, J. H.
Arjona, John
Arjona, L. M. S.
Ashton-Warner, Sylvia
Astle, Melvin J.
ASTM-TAPPI Symposium on Petroleum Waxes
Aston, John G.
Aston, Melvin J.
Bartlett, John, 1820-1905, comp.
Bastiat, Frédéric, 1801-1850
Ben' Ary, Ruth
Benary-Isbert, Margot
Berdiaev, Nikolai Aleksandrovich, 1874-1948
Birket-Smith, Kaj, 1893-
Bowker (R.R.) Company, firm, publishers, New York
Boyd, James
Boyd, J. P.
Boyd, Malcolm
Boyle, Andrew

Boyle, Hon, Robert, 1627-1691
Burton, Sir Richard Francis, 1821-1890, tr.
Castellanos Velasco, Francisco
Cecil, Lord David, 1902-
Československá akademie věd
Charles, Alfred Chalmers
Charles de Jesus, Pere
Charles d'Orléans, 1394-1465
Charles, duke of Cornwall, 1948-
Charles V, duke of Lorraine, 1643-1690
Charles Edward, the Young Pretender, 1720-1788
Charles V, emperor of Germany SEE ...
Charles V, emperor of the Holy Roman Empire, 1500-1558
Charles VI, king of France, 1368-1422
Charles VIII, king of France, 1470-1498
Charles I, king of Great Britain, 1600-1649
Charles I, king of Great Britain, 1600-1649, defendant
Charles II, king of Great Britain, 1630-1685
Charles XII, king of Sweden, 1682-1718
Charles, Robert Henry, 1855-1931
Charles, Robert Henry, 1882-
Ch'ên, Jerome
Chi, Wen-shun, ed. Readings in Chinese Communist documents
Chi, Wen-shun. Technology in China
Chiang Kai-shek
Chicago. University. Law School
Churchill, Sir Winston Leonard Spencer
Conference on Poverty-in-Plenty: the Poor in Our Affluent Society
Conference on Unemployment and the American Economy
D, George
Daalder, Hans
Dabbs, Jack
D'Abreu, Gerald
Dabrowski, Kazimierz
Da C. Andrade, E.
Da Cal, Ernesto
D'A Cennini, Cennino
D'Achery, Luc
Dack, Gail
Da Costa Edwardo, Octavio
Da Costa, Felix
Dacso, Michael
Daedalus

Dal, Erik
Daland, Geneva
Dale, Alan
Dal Fabbro, Mario
Dalldorf, Gilbert
D'Allemagne, Henry
Dal Nogare, Stephen
D'Alonzo
Dametz, Max
D'Amico, Victor
Damion, Steve
D'Amour, Fred
Dampier, William
Daniel, Walter
Daniell, David
Daniel-Rops, Henry
Da Ponte, Lorenzo
Darby
D'Arcy, Eric
Darcy, H. L.
D'Arcy, Martin
Dardarian, Leo
D'Ardenne, S. R.
D'Areangelo, Amelio
Darzins, Egons
Das, Bhaganan
Das, Daisy
Dasein, Arthur
Das-Gupta, A. K.
Das Gupta, Askin
Da Silva, John
Dasman, Raymond
Das, Tulsi
David-Neel, Alexandra
Davies-Rodgers, Ellen
Da Vinci, Leonardo
D'Azzo, John
De Alarcon, Pedro
Dean, Howard E.
Deane, Shirley
De Angeli, Arthur C.
Dearborn, Terry H.
De Armand, David W.

Dearmer, Percy
Deatherage, George
Deb, Paul
De Baca, Carlos
De Barr, A. E.
Debicki
De Blij, Harm J.
De Boer, Julius
Debrix, Louis
Debye, Peter
De Camp, Lyon S.
Decarlo, V. J.
De Fleur, Melvin
Defoe, Daniel
Defoe, Louis
De Ford, Miriam
De Grazia, Edward
De Kruif, Paul Henry
De L Ryals, Clyde
De La Barco, P.
De La Brete, Jean
De La Mare, P. B. D.
De La Mare, Walter
De La Roche, Maza
Del Bagno, Panuccio
Delbo, Charlotte
Del Bo, Dino
De Leiris
Delgado, Roy
De L'Isle-Adams, P.
Delitzsch, Franz
Dellabella, Stefano
Della-Piana, Gabriel
Della Valle, Gustave
Delling, Gerhard
Delli Quadri, Fred
De Los Rios, Giver
De Losingo, Herbert
Del Rio, Amelia
Del Vecchio, Alfred
Delzell, Charles
De Man, Paul
De Mille, Agnes

Denaro, Eric
De Nault, Martin
Denberg, Fred
Den Boer, James
Denes, Gabor
D'Enes, Tibor
Den Hartog, Jacob
Denholm-Young, Noel
De Puy, Charles
Depuy, Ernest
De Quincey, Thomas
De Rachewiltz
Der Beets, Richard
Der Ziel, John
De Saint Laurent
De Saint Pierre
De Saint-Exupery
De Saint-Pierre, Michel
De Saint-Simon, Louis
De Sola, Ralph
D'Espezel, Pierre
De Vane, William Clyde
De Voto, Bernard Augustine, 1897-1955
De Vries, Peter
D'Eye, R. W. M.
D, H
D. H. Victor
Dice, Stanley
Di Certo, Polaris
Dicesare, Louis
Di Chiro, Giovanni
D'Isa, Frank
D La Palme, William
Dobrée, Bonamy, 1891-
Dodgson, Charles Lutwidge
D'Orbigny, Alcide
Dos Passos, John, 1896-
Du Bois, Cora Alice, 1903-
Du Bois, William Edward Burghardt, 1868-1963
Duly, Leslie
Dumas, Alexander
Du Maurier, Daphne
Dumery, Henry

Du Mesnil Marrizny, Jules
Dumit, Edward
Du Porte, Andre
Du Praw, Edward
Dupraw, Ernest
Du Pre, Flint
Dupre, Howard
Dupuy, Richard Ernest, 1887-
Duvoism, Roger
Du Vries, Henri
Duwaji, Ghazi
D Wolf, John
Eisenhower, Dwight David
Elkins, William
Elk-Nes, Frank
Elkouri, Edna
Ellis, Willis
Ellis-Fermour, Una
Ellison, Alfred
Elonka, Steve
El'Piner, Albert
Elrick, George
Elsgolc, Albert
El' Sogol' ts, Henry
Elton, Godfrey Elton
Fite, Gilbert Courtland
Fitz, Thomas
Fitze, Kenneth
Fitzgerald, Charles
Fitz Gerald, Edward
Fitz Gerald, Henry
Fitz-Gerald, John
Fitzgerel, Robert
Fitz Gibbon, Constantine
Fitzgibbon, Russell
Fonagy, Ivan
Fon Eisen, Anthony
Fon Elisen, Anthony T.
Foner, Philip
Formon, Samuel
Foundation for Economic Education, Inc.
Francesco d' Assisi, Saint

Franco-American Colloquium
Fuentes, Patricia de
Gale Research Company
Gaulle, Charles de
Gide, André Paul Guillaume
Goethe, Johann Wolfgang von
Granville-Barker, Harley Granville
H.
Hailey, William Malcolm Hailey
Hall, Edward
Hall Williams, John
Halladay, Anne
Hallam, William
Hall-Edwards, Paul
Halliwell, Leslie
Halliwell-Philipps, James
Hallman, Victor
Hall-Quest, Olga
Halls, Geraldine
Hamburger, Joseph
Harvard University. American Defense, Harvard Groups
Harvard University. Class of 1898
Harvard University. Class of 1930
Harvard University. Class of 1946
Harvard University. Computation Laboratory
H. E.
Henry
Henry, A. F.
Henry, Carl
Henry, Carl, 1891-1947
Henry, Charles
Henry, Charles, pseud. ("pseud." is disregarded in filing)
Henry College, Campbell, Tex.
Henry, C. W.
Henry, Sir David
Henry, David A.
Henry, Duke of Lancaster, 1299?-1361
Henry E. Huntington Library and Art Gallery
Henry VII, Earl of Richmond
Henry, Sir Edward Richard, bart., 1850-1931
Henry, Father, 1881-1939
Henry Ford Hospital Symposium

Henry Ford trade school, Dearborn, Mich.
Henry Frederick, Duke of Cumberland, 1745-1790, defendant
Henry, George, tr.
Henry, George A.
Henry, George Adams
Henry, G. W.
Henry, Mrs. Jennie (Dow), 1885
Henry I, King of England
Henry II, King of England
Henry VIII, King of England, 1491-1547
Henry II, King of Scotland
Henry, VIII, King of the House of Tudor
Henry, Mr.
Henry, O.
Henry, O. B.
Henry, O. D., 1921-
Henry of Avranches, 13th Cent.
Henry of Blois
Henry of Flanders
Henry of Huntingdon, 1084?-1155
Henry of Silegrave
Henry, Paul
Henry, Paul 1857-
Henry, Paul 1896-
Henry, Paul Emile
Henry, Pierre 1903-
Henry, Pierre 1906-
Henry, Professor
Henry Raspe
Henry Raspe, David
Henry street settlement, New York
Henry the Black
Henry, the Minstrel, 15th cent.
Henry, the Minstrel, fl. 1470-1492
Henry, William
Henry, W. O.
Henry-Greard, O.
Henry-Lacaze, Lydie
Henryson, Robert
Henschel, Stan
Homerus
H. W.

Kingdom, Thomas
King-Hall, Stephen
Kingman, Lee
Laas, William
Labaree, Leonard
La Baume, Peter
La Feber, Walter
Lafener, Minard
La Fontaine, Jean de, 1621-1695
L'Amour, Louis
La Violette, Forrest
Ld' Amat, Roman
Le Bar, Lois
Lebel, Robert
Lebon, Robert
Le Clerc, Frederic
Leclerc, Gerald
Le Clerc, Ivor
Lemarchand, René
Le Nain De Tillemont, Louis
L'Engle, Madeleine
Le Sage, Laurent
Le Shan, Eda J.
Les Tina, Dorothy
L-Estrange, Alfred
L' Estrange, Robert
Lestz, Gerald
Le Sueur, William
Lettis, Richard
Lévi-Strauss, Claude
L' Hote, Jean
Li, Jerome
Liacos, Paul
Life (Chicago)
Li Yu, Jon Pu Tuan
Lo, Arthur
Lo, Kung

Loades, Marcus
Lo Cicero, Donald
Lo Pinto, Maria
L'Orange, Hans
Los Angeles County Museum
Losch, August
Los Rios, G. G.
Lossky, Andrew
Louis, pseud.
Louis, A.
Louis Alexander, Prince of Battenberg SEE ...
Louis, Andrew, 1907-
Louis Bonaparte, King of Holland, 1778-1846
Louis I de France, King of Naples, 1339-1384
Louis, Duke of Burgundy, dauphin of France, 1682-1712
Louis II, Emperor, King of Italy, 822(ca.)-875
Louis, Father
Louis Ferdinand, Prince of Prussia, 1907-
Louis Francis, Prince of Battenberg
Louis, Henry
Louis XI, King of France, 1423-1483
Louis XII, King of France, 1462-1515
Louis XIII, King of France, 1601-1643
Louis XIV, King of France, 1638-1715
Louis XV, King of France, 1710-1774
Louis XVI, King of France, 1754-1793
Louis XVI, King of France, 1754-1793, defendant
Louis XVIII, King of France, 1755-1824
Louis I, King of Germany
Louis Marie Philippe, Prince of Orleans and Branganqa SEE ...
Louis, of Toulouse, Saint bp. SEE ...
Louis Paul, pseud.
Louis, Prince of Orleans, 1878
Louis, Prince of Orleans and Branganqa, 1878-1920
Louis, the German, King of the East Franks SEE ...
Louis-Andre
Louis-Frederic, pseud.
Louis-Marie, pere
Louis-Marie, pere, 1896-
M' SEE ALSO Mac, Mc
M. Robert Gomberg Memorial Conference
Mabry, Marion

Mac SEE ALSO Mc, M'
Mac Adams, Howard
Macalaster, Andrews
Mac Alpine
Macatee, J. Edward
Macaulay, Wallace
Mac Donald, Donald
Mac Ginitie, George
Macginitie, Phyllis
Machiavelli, Niccoló, 1469-1527
Madariaga, Salvador de, 1886-
Madden, Robert
Magill, Frank Northern, 1907-
Mao, James
Mao Tsê-Tung
Ma'Oz, Moske
Map, Walter
Martin, Albert
Martin-Barbaz, Samuel
Martindale, Andrew
Martin-Doyle, John
Martins, Jose
Martin-Santos, Luis
Mary
Mary Aquinas, Sister
Mary Naomi, Sister
Mary of Bethlehem
Mary Oliver, Mother
Mary Pauline, Sister
Mary Rose Eileen, Sister
Mary Ursula Cooper, Sister
Mary Xaveria, Sister
Maryknoll Sisters
Maryland State Department of Health
Maryon, Herbert
Mary-Rousseliére, Guy
Mayer, Allan
Mazur, Paul
Mc SEE ALSO Mac, M'
Mc Adam, John
McClellan, James Edward
Mc Cormick, James

Mc Gee, Barbara
Mc Gee, Charles
Mc Gregor, Craig
McKay, Ernest A.
McNall, Preston Essex, 1888-
Mc Williams, Robert
Mead, Emerson
Michigan. University. Center for Research on Conflict Resolution
Misyurkeyen, I. .
M. I. T. SEE Massachusetts Institute of Technology
Mitau, G. Theodore
M'Lane, Charles
M'Laren, J. T.
Mlotkowski, Casimir
M'Neile, A. H.
M'Nelly, Theodore
Moak, Helen
Montherlant, Henri de, 1896-
Moon, Samuel, ed.
Morón, Guillermo
Mueller SEE ALSO Muller
Mueller, Bernard
Muller SEE ALSO Mueller
Muller, Edward J.
Murasaki, Shikibu, b. 978?
The Nation (New York)
Neely, Wayne
Ne'Eman
Neer, May
New, Chester W.
New England Nuclear Corporation, Boston
New, John F. H.
New Orleans Parents' Council
New Republic
New York. Bellevue hospital
New York (City) Board of Education
New York (Colony)
New York (Colony) Laws, statutes, etc.
New York (County) Courthouse
New York County Lawyers Association
New York Herald Tribune
New York Institute of Technology

New York. Public Library
New York School of Social Work
New York (State)
New York (State) Agricultural experiment station, Geneva
New York (State) Department of health
New York. State Library, Albany
New York. State Library school, Albany
New York. Stock exchange
New York Times
New York Times Book Review
New York University
New Yorker
Newark, New Jersey
Niclas, Yolla
Nic Leodhas, Sorche
Niclson, Marjorie
Nicolson, Sir Harold George, 1886-1968
Nkrumah, Kwame, Pres. Ghana. 1909-
Nowell-Smith, Simon Harcourt, 1909-
Oakberg, James
O'Anderson, Keith
Obaid, Antonio
O'Ballance, Edgar
Obourn, Ellsworth
O'Brady, Frédéric
Obregon, Mauricio
O'Brian, Frank
O'Brian, John
Obrucher, William
O'Bryne, Roscoe
Obukar, Charles
O'Callaghass, Denis
Ocampo, Victoria
O'Casey, Sean
Ochsner, Alton
Ocon, Ralph
O'Connell, Ann
O'Connell, Charles
O'Connor, William Van, 1915
Odeh, Peter
O'Dell, Albert
Odell, Carol

Saintine, X. B.
Saintsbury, George
Saint-Simon, Claude
Saint-Simon, Henri
Saint-Vallier, Jean
Sainz, Gustavo
Saisselin, Rémy G.
Scientific American
Scole, Leo
Scott, Sir Walter, bart., 1771-1832
Smith, Arthur J., 1850-1915
Smith, Arthur J., 1850-1923
Smith, Samuel
Smith, Samuel, 1584?-1662?
Smith, Samuel, 1720-1776
Smith, Samuel, 1836-1906
Smith, Samuel, 1904-
Smith, Samuel Abbot
Snow, Sir Charles Percy, 1905-
Srole, Leo
St. SEE ALSO Saint
St. Clair, Robert
St. Johns, Adela Rogers
St. Martin, Georges
St. Vincent, Edwin
Staack, Hagen
Sun Yat-sen
Tempaki, Ralph
Ten Broek, Jacobus
Tenbroek, Jacobus A.
Tenbrook, Robert
Tensen, Ruth
Teodorovich, G. I.
Te Paske, John
Teper, Lazare
Ter Brugge, A. J.
Ter Haar, Dirk
Ter-Pogossian, Michel
Thomas, A.
Thomas, Adolphe
Thomas a' Kempis
Thomas Alva Edison Foundation Institute, 7th

Thomas Aquinas, saint
Thomas, Charles
Thomas, de Burton
Thomas, de Cantimpré
Thomas de Strasbourg
Thomas, earl of Lancaster
Thomas Iron Company
Thomas, Norman
Thomas of Celano, Brother
Thomas of Elmham
Thomas, Owen
Thomas, Winburn T.
Tolstoǐ, Lev Nikolaevich, graf, 1828-1910. Anna Karenina
Tolstoǐ, Lev Nikolaevich, graf, 1828-1910. War and Peace
Tovey, Sir Donald Francis, 1875-1940
Trevor-Roper, Hugh Redwald
Twentieth Century Fund
U, Htin Aung
Ubbelohode, Alfred
Ubben, Earl
Uhley, Herman
Unamuno y Jugo, Miguel de, 1864-1936
United Nations
United Nations. Department of Public Information
United Nations. Statistical Office
United Press International
United States SEE ALSO U. S.
United States Air Force
United States. Army
United States, Army air forces, 4th fighter group
United States War Dept.
Unity School of Christianity
Urwin, Kathleen M.
U. S. SEE ALSO United States
U. S. Armed Forces
U. S. Army
U. S. Army, A. E. F., 1917-1920. 1st Division
U. S. Army, A. E. F., 1917-1920. 2nd Division
U. S. Army Air Forces
U. S. Army Air Forces. 7th Air Force
U. S. Army Air Forces. 8th Air Force
U. S. Army Air Forces. 8th Air Force. 25th Bombardment Group

U. S. Army Air Forces. 8th Air Force. 71st Bombardment Group
U. S. Army Air Forces. 8th Air Force. 19th Fighter Wing
U. S. Army Air Forces. Air Service Command
U. S. Army Air Forces. 5th Bombardment Division
U. S. Army Air Forces. 3d Bombardment Group
U. S. Army Air Forces. 305th Bombardment Group
U. S. Army Air Forces. 303d Bombardment Group (Heavy)
U. S. Army Air Forces. 14th Bombardment Squadron
U. S. Army Air Forces. 9th Bombardment Wing
U. S. Army Air Forces. 3d Bombardment Wing (Heavy)
U. S. Army Air Forces. Flying Training Command
U. S. Army Air Forces. 80th Interceptor Control Squadron
U. S. Army Air Forces. Office of Flying Safety
U. S. Army. Alaskan Command
U. S. Army and Navy Munitions Board
U. S. Army. 184th Antiaircraft Artillery Battalion
U. S. Army. 387th Antiaircraft Artillery Battalion
U. S. Army. 50th Antiaircraft Artillery Brigade
U. S. Army. Army, Pacific
U. S. Army. 1st Cavalry
U. S. Army. 3d Cavalry
U. S. Army. 1st Cavalry (Colored)
U. S. Army. 1st Cavalry Division
U. S. Army. 1st Cavalry (Volunteer)
U. S. Army. Continental Army
U. S. Army. II Corps
U. S. Army. IV Corps
U. S. Army. Corps of Engineers
U. S. Army. 35th Division
U. S. Army. 44th Division
U. S. Army. Eighth Army
U. S. Army. First Army
U. S. Army Map Service
U. S. Congress
U. S. 1st Congress, 1789-1791
U. S. 1st Congress, 1789-1791. House
U. S. 1st Congress, 1789-1791. Senate
U. S. 1st Congress, 1st session, 1789
U. S. 1st Congress, 1st session, 1789. House
U. S. 1st Congress, 2d session, 1789. House
U. S. 1st-2d Congress, 1789-1793
U. S. 40th Congress, 1867-1869

U. S. 63d Congress, 1913-1915
U. S. 63d Congress, 1st session, 1913
U. S. 63d Congress, 2d session, 1913-1914
U. S. 85th Congress, 1st session 1957
U. S. 85th Congress, 2d session, 1958
U. S. 85th Congress, 2d session, 1958. House
U. S. 85th Congress, 2d session, 1958. Senate
U. S. Congress. Aviation Policy Board
U. S. Congress. Conference Committees, 1919-1920
U. S. Congress. Conference Committees, 1956
U. S. Congress. Conference Committees, 1957
U. S. Congress. Conference Committees, 1962
U. S. Congress. House
U. S. Congress. Joint Economic Committee
U. S. Congress. Senate
U. S. Congress. Senate. Special Committee on Aging
U. S. Constitution
U. S. Court of Military Appeals
U. S. Courts
U. S. Department of State. Historical Office
U. S. Department of State. Office of Public Affairs
U. S. President's Commission for the Observance of Human Rights
    Year 1968
U. S. Supreme Court
U. S. Surgeon General, Advisory Committee
U. S. War Dept.
Usborne, Richard
Usher, Esther
Valmiki
Van Abbe, Derek
Vanable, Joseph
Vanags, Alexander
Van Arsdel, Wallace B.
Vance, B. Bernarr
Vance, John
Van De Loo, K. J.
Van De Luyster, Nelson
Vandell, Robert F.
Van Dellin, Robert
Van Demark, Paul
Van Den Barren, Charles
Van Den Berghe, Pierre

Vanden, Brock
Vander, Francis
Van Der Haas, Haas
Vander, Haeghen
Van Der Heyde, Morton
Vander Plas, Leendert
Van Der Plas, Michel
Vanderbilt, Amy
Van Deusen, Glyndon Garlock, 1897-
Van Doren, Carl Clinton, 1885-1950
Van Tassel, David
Van' T Hoff, J. H.
Van Thompson, Paul
Van Wormer, Joe
Vera, James
Ver Brugghen, Adrien
Ver Steeg, Clarence
Verwer, Hans
Von Der Osten, Hans
Vondra, Jiri
Von Gierke, Otto
Von Hagen, Victor Wolfgang, 1908-
Washington Academy of Science
Washington, Allyn
Washington, D. C.
Washington, D. C. Textile Museum
Washington, George
The Washington Kiplinger Editors
Washington (State) Governor's Council on Aging
Washington University
Wharton, Edith Newbold (Jones) 1862-1937
Wheeler-Bennett, John Wheeler, 1902-
Wisconsin. State Historical Society
Woolf, Virginia (Stephen) 1882-1941
Zeno, pseud.
Zullner, Hans
Zuman, Paul
Zum Winkel, Hans J.
Zum Winkel, H. J.
Zurita, Alonso de, b. 1511 or 12

TITLE CARDS

<u>A</u>, a Novel by Andy Warhol
A & b & c of English Usage   (A a<u>n</u>d...)
"A" and "B" <u>M</u>andates
A & <u>P</u>
A & <u>s</u> & p & T - i OP & b Index of Current Taxonomic Research
A. <u>B</u>ronson Alcott
The A <u>C</u>ompany
A <u>f</u>or Effort
A. <u>G</u>ellii
A <u>I</u>s for Advent
A <u>I</u>s for A<u>p</u>ple
A, <u>O</u>ne to Twelve
A <u>to</u> Z SEE ALSO A-Z
A <u>to</u> Z
A <u>W</u>as a Leader
A<u>a</u>ron Burr conspiracy
A<u>as</u>a Code of Ethics
A<u>AU</u>N
A <u>B</u> Bookman's Yearbook
A. B. <u>F</u>rost Book
A. B. <u>G</u>ray Report
A. B. <u>S</u>impson
Ab <u>U</u>rbe Condita
AB<u>A</u>
Aba<u>c</u>us Arithmetic
AB<u>C</u> Book
A B C B<u>u</u>nny
A. B. C., <u>M</u>adrid
A B C <u>of</u> Barbecue
The AB<u>C</u> of <u>C</u>ollecting
A B C of <u>L</u>ettering
A. B. C. of <u>M</u>usic   (Disregard periods)
A B C of <u>M</u>usic
A. B. C. <u>P</u>rograms
ABC <u>S</u>horthand
A B C'<u>s</u> of Antennas
A B C's of <u>C</u>hemistry
ABC's of <u>G</u>lass
A B C's of <u>the</u> Stock Market
A-B-<u>S</u>kis

A-C Carrier Control Systems
A-C Machines
A C Machines
Achilles the Donkey
A C I Manual of Concrete
Acid Nightmare
Acid Test
Acid-Base Equilibria
Acids & Bases
Ad
Ad Hoc Diplomat
Ada & the Wild Duck
Adam
Adam & Eve
Adam and Jefferson
Adam and the Wolf
Adam-Jefferson Letters
Adam's Ancestors
Adam's Atoms
Adams Federalists
Ad-Libs
Ad-Maze
Advances in radio research
The advantages of dark
Advantages of the small local church
Adventure in Liberty
The adventure into thought
An adventure with people
A. E. Housman
"A"-14   ("A"-Fourteen)
African one-party states
.a G A R D Flight test Manual
A G. K. Chesterton omnibus
A-Going to the Westward
A. H. Reed
A. L. A.
Algebraic Curves
A. M.
AM - FM Broadcast Maintenance
AM - FM - TV Alignment
A. M. Mackay Pioneer Missionary
A M A

Anthropologists in the Field
Anthropology Today
Anti-Anthropomorphism
Antibiotic-Producing Microscopic Fungi
Antibiotics
Antibodies & Immunity
Anticancer Agents
Anticapitalistic Mentality
Anti-Christianity of Kierkegaard
Anticoagulants and Fibrinolycins
Anti-Corn Law League
Anti-Death League
Antifederalist papers
Antigone & Selected Poems
Anti-Memoirs
Anti-Poverty Programs
Antiquary
Antique & Classic Cars
Antique Automobiles
Antique Views of Boston
Antiqueno Colonization in Western Colombia
Antiques and Bygones
Antiques as an Investment
Anti-Semite and Jew
Antitrust Analysis
Anti-Trust Policy
Antiworlds
Antiworlds and the Fifth Ace
Antoine & the Theatre-Libre
A-Priori Information & Time Series Analysis
A R R L Antenna Book
Auden's poetry
A-V Instruction
La aventura equivocial de lope de
A. W. Tozer
Awake and sing
A-Z SEE ALSO A to Z
The Azores
Aztec Temple
Baker's dictionary of theology
Best magazine articles
The Bible and the Church

The Bible book by book
Bible. Danish. 1911
Bible. English. 1901. American Revised
Bible. English. 1948. Authorized
Bible. English. 1957. Authorized
Bible. English. 1961. New English
Bible. English. 1955. Revised Standard
The Bible in Milton's epics
Bible. Italian. 1471
Bible. Latin. 1913
Bible legend books
Bible: Myth or reality?
Bible. N. T. Apocryphal books. Acts
Bible. N. T. Apocryphal books. English
Bible. N. T. English
Bible. N. T. Ephesians
Bible. N. T. I Corinthians   (...first...)
Bible. N. T. I John
Bible. N. T. I Peter
Bible. N. T. Galatians
Bible. N. T. Gospels
Bible. N. T. Gospels. English
Bible. N. T. Greek
Bible. N. T. Revelation
Bible. N. T. II Corinthians
Bible. N. T. II John
Bible. N. T. Spanish
Bible. N. T. III John
The Bible on the world
The Bible on vacation and election
The Bible or evolution
Bible. O. T. Amos
Bible. O. T. English
Bible. O. T. Esther
Bible. O. T. Exodus
Bible. O. T. I Chronicles
Bible. O. T. I Chronicles. English. 1965
Bible. O. T. Greek. 1821
Bible. O. T. Greek. 1906
Bible. O. T. Pentateuch
Bible. O. T. Psalms
Bible. O. T. II Chronicles

Bible. O. T. Syriac
Bible. O. T. Zechariah
Bible Personalities
Bible, religion, and the public schools
Biblical archaeology
The blue pavilion
The Book of the States
BPR annual cumulative
Cassell's encyclopaedia of world literature
Cassell's Spanish dictionary
Charles I and Cromwell
Charles I at Corisbrooke
Charles I, king of Sweden
Charles II
Charles II and the Cavalier House of Commons
Charles II Domestic Silver
Charles II, king of France
Charles II, king of Sweden
The Chronicles of America Series, v. 33
The Chronicles of America Series, v. 37
The Chronicles of America Series, v. 52
The Chronicles of America Series, v. 55
The Chronicles of America Series, v. 56
The Clark lectures, Trinity College, Cambridge University, 1944
Collected Essays
Collected Poems
Color SEE ALSO Colour
Color and design
Color television
Colorful world of Babar
Colossus and other poems
Colour SEE ALSO Color
Colour guide to clouds
Colour vision
Colours of Clarity
Colt automatic pistols
El concierto de San Ovidio
Conference on Verbal Learning and Verbal Behavior
C. R. C. standard mathematic tables
Cross-country techniques illustrated
A Cycle of Cathay
Dawn of Conscience

Day of Doom
DC-AC Laboratory Manual
DC-3   (DC-three)
Dead Sea Scrolls
...Debate index...
Definition of God
Definition of Good
De Gaulle and the world
Delectable Past
De Lee's Obstetrics for Nurses
De Lesseps: Builder of the Suez
Delinquency and Child Guidance
De Menil collection
Demetrios of Greece
Les deux poemes de la folie tristan
DNA: At the Core of Life Itself
D-99
Dock brief and other plays
Doctor SEE ALSO Dr.
Doctor Alone Can't Cure You
Doctor Zhivago
Doctors as Men of Letters
Double O Seven SEE OO Seven
"Double profit" in Macbeth
Downtown U. S. A.
Dr. SEE ALSO Doctor
Dr. Albert Schweitzer, Medical Missionary
Dr. Spock talks with Mothers
Dracula
Draft and the Vietnam War
The El Agheila Battle Town
The El Capitan Peak
Elden Mountain Story
The Elephant that went astray
El Paso   (El treated as prefix when part of a name)
The Encyclopedia of jazz
The Encyclopedia of mental Health
Encyclopedia of modern architecture
...Les enfants terribles
Engineers unlimited
Engines and trains
England and the Near East

English historical documents
Englishe dogges
Englishman
Englishmen and others
Enigma of drug addiction
Equality
Every Artist His Own Scandal
Every Day a Surprise
Every Day by Storm
Every Day in the Year
Every Man's Brother
Every Time I Climb a Tree
Everyboddy's Friend
Everybody Call Me Father
Everyday Animals
Every-Day Book
Everyday Devotions for Youth
Everyday Wildflowers
Everyman's Classical atlas
Every-Member Evangelism
Everything to Live For
Ezra, Nehemiah
F. Scott Fitzgerald
Fayette County Cemetery Inscriptions
FBI in Peace and War
Feast of Fear
The Federalist
Feiffer's Album
F-86 Sabre
First American
I & II Thessalonians
1st Nine Months of Life
First 125 Years
40+1
Forty Poems and Stories
The Fox from his lair
France: 1814-1919
France in the Nineteenth Century
France in the 16th Century
French: 3100 Steps of Master Vocabulary
French Wars of Religion
Funk & Wagnalls standard dictionary of folklore...

Hand Analysis
Hand and Foot
Hand & Machine
Hand and machine woodwork
Hand book SEE ALSO Handbook
Hand Book for History Teachers
Hand book for telescope making
Hand Book of Abbreviations
Hand Decorating Projects
Hand in Glove
Hand Made Jewelry
A Hand on my shoulder
Hand upon the time
Hand woodworking tools
Handball
Handbook SEE ALSO Hand book
Handbook & Charting Manual
Handbook for Beginning Debaters
A handbook for modelling
Hand-Book for Travellers
A handbook of general knowledge
Handbook of mathematical tables
Hand-book of Proverbs
Hand-Built Pottery
Handcrafts simplified
Hand-List of Bede Manuscripts
Hand-List of Turkish...
Hand-Me-Down House
Hand-Taming Wild Birds
Hand-to-Hand Combat
Handwork done by children
Hand-work methods of...
Handwork of surgery
A handwriting manual
Handy man of the year
Handy man wanted
Handy-man of the year
Handy-man wanted
Henry Adams and Brooks Adams
Henry and the astronaut
Henry Barnard on Education
Henry Bly and other Plays

Henry Cabot Lodge: A biography
Henry of Newark
Henry of Portugal
Henry: Play
Henry Purcell and the Restoration Theatre
Henry Purcell, 1659-1695: Essays on His Music   (Sixteen fifty-
    nine to sixteen ninety-five: Essays on...)
Henry Purcell, Sixteen Fifty-nine to Sixteen Ninety-five: His Life...
Henry Sloane Coffin
Henry VIII   (Henry the eighth)
Henry VIII, and his times   (Henry the eighth, and his times)
Henry VIII, and Luther   (Henry the eighth, and Luther)
Henry VIII and the Lutherans
Henry VIII, and the Reformation   (Henry the eighth and the reforma-
    tion)
Henry the Explorer
Henry V   (Henry the fifth)
Henry V, and the Invasion of France   (Henry the fifth, and the Inva-
    sion of France)
Henry IV   (Henry the fourth)
Henry the Navigator
Henry II, the Vanquished King   (Henry the second the Vanquished
    King)
HENRY VII   (Henry the seventh)
Henry, the smiling dog
Henry Watkins Allen of Louisiana
Henry's Busy Winter
Henry's Lincoln
Her Majesty's Customs and Excise
How to make $
Idylls of Theokritos
I E Review
IEE News
IEEE Proceedings
IEEE Spectrum
IEEE Transactions
If the Shoe Fits
Information please
Introduction to Astronomy
Introduction to Geometry
An Introduction to the English Novel
Iowa Whittlings

I. P. A. Review
Ipcress File
A Lady in Boomtown
Louis of Granada
Louis of Toulouse
Louis Philippe and the July Monarchy
Louis Sullivan
Louis XV   (... the fifteenth)
Louis XIV
Louis XIV and the Greatness of France
Louis XIV at Versailles
Louis XIV of France
Louis IX of France
Louis XVI
Louis XVI Furniture
Louis-Philippe: "Citizen King"
A Love Affair with the Law
LSD, man & society
M. & M. Karolik collection of eighteenth century American Arts
M is for monster
Ma and Pa Hilton
Ma princesse cherie
MAA problem book II
Mabel the whale
Le Malade imaginaire
Mannerism and habit
Man's best friend
Mansion in the sky
Minnesota studies in the philosophy of science
Mistakes in Geometric proofs
Mister SEE ALSO Mr.
Mister Andrews School
Mister Fisherman
Mistral
Mistress SEE ALSO Mrs.
Mistress Malapert
MLA international bibliography
M. N. Roy's mission to China
Mozart handbook
Mozart: His character, his work
Mozart: the man and his work
Mozart's Librettos

Mozart's Operas
Mr. SEE ALSO Mister
Mr. Roosevelt's Four Freedoms
Mr. Willowby's Christmas Tree
Mrs. SEE ALSO Mistress
Mrs. Beeton's Family Cookery
M-26   (M-twenty-six)
Much Ado about Nothing
Nemo Meets the Emperor
Neo-African literature
Neolithic Culture
New Arithmetic
New Japanese Architecture
New Testament In Modern English
New York
New York State
The New York times sports almanac
New Zealand Plants
Newark
Newborn child
1914 Diary   (Nineteen Fourteen Diary)
1919   (Nineteen Nineteen)
Nineteen twenties
O. Henry Almanac
O. Henry Stories
Oars, Sails, and Steam
OAS and the United Nations
...On music and musicians
1/2 is Mine   (One half is Mine)
One Hundred & One
One Hundred Blackboard Games
150 Brief Sermon Outlines   (One hundred fifty...)
101 Puzzles   (One hundred one puzzles)
1,000,000 centuries   (one million...)
1800 Riddles   (One thousand eight...)
1001 Answers to Questions About Trees
One Thousand Questions and Answers
1234 Modern End-game Studies
One thousand years on Mound Key
1,2,3 - Infinity
One World
007   (0 0 Seven)

007 James Bond   (0 0 Seven James Bond)
Oodles of Noodles
Open and Closed Mind
Oxford history of English literature, v. 3
Oxford history of English literature, v. 5
El Paso, the City of Pleasure SEE El Paso (Elpaso)
Pearl
The + and − of gambling
Possum Moods
Post Apollo Space Exploration
Post Communication
Post Mortem
Post Mortem Examination of Ruminants
Post Office Clerk-Carrier
Post Office Department
Post Operative Cardiac Care
Post Painterly Abstraction
Post True Stories of Courage
Postage Stamps
Postal Clerk-Carrier Exams
Post-Conciliar Nun
Post-Entry Training
Post-Graduate Lectures
Postmaster, Fourth Class
Post-Mortem Appearances
Post-Operative Chest
Post-Operative Complications
Post-Paleozoic
Post-Ramessid Remains
Post-Victoria Britain
Post-War Britain
Postwar Economic Growth
Post-war Immigrants in Canada
Postwar Trade in Divided Germany
Post-War Years
Postwar Years
Pre-calculus mathematics; a programmed text
Der Prozess um des esels Schatten
Rock to Riches
Rock 2000
Rock Women
Rockefeller Center

Saint SEE ALSO St.
Saint among Savages
Saint Augustine on Personality
Saint in Hyde Park
Saint James in Spain
Saint Just: Apostle of the Terror
Saint Nicholas and the Tub
Saint of Ardent Desires
Saint Thomas and the Unconscious Mind
Sainte-Boune to Baudelaire
Sainte-John Perse
Saintmaker's Christmas Eve
Saints: Adventures in Courage
Saints and Scholars
Sam & Son Returns
... Sangre y arena
Sets, relations & functions
The 7 Lively Arts
...And shed a bitter tear
St. SEE ALSO Saint
St. John's Easter Office
St. Louis Movement in Philosophy
Stability amid change
The statesman's year-book
Statistics sources
Stevens' poetry of thought
Survey of progress in chemistry
Ten % chance to live
... and then I told the President
Thoreau: A Writer's Journal
Thoreau Handbook
Thoreau: Man of Concord
A Tribute
T. S. Eliot, the metaphysical perspective
12½ Main Street   (Twelve and One half Main Street)
12:30 From Croydon   (Twelve thirty...)
The XXth Century   (Twentieth century)
XXth century health and pleasure resorts
Twentieth Century Russia
20th Century Stage Decoration
XXth Century Young People
Twentieth-Century Music

20th-century plays in synopsis
20th-century teenagers
Twenty four new country dances...
Twenty Grand Short Stories
20,000,000 Tons Under the Sea   (Twenty Million Tons...)
Twenty Prose Poems
20,000 Leagues Under the Sea   (Twenty thousand...)
Twenty Years at Hull-House
24 short stories   (Twenty-four...)
29 Stories   (Twenty-nine...)
Two hundred fifty years of Quakerism...
... 295 American birds   (two hundred ninety...)
201 French Verbs   (Two Hundred One French Verbs)
222 photographic views of...   (Two hundred twenty-two...)
200 ways to reduce engineering and...
2 + 2 = 3
United Methodist Profile
United States   SEE ALSO   U. S.   (as Us)
United States and Cuba
United States, 1830-1850
United States Government organization manual
United States In Vietnam
United States Treaties
United States vs. United Shoe Corporation   (United States versus...)
United States War Medals
Up Against the Wall
Urban Neighborhood
U. S.   SEE ALSO   United States
U. S. Air Force in Space
U. S. Colonial History
Us or Them War
U. S. Trade Policy
U. S. A. Since the First World War
Usage and Abusage
Use and Misuse of Drugs
U. S. S. R.
USSR: A Concise History
USSR Arms the Third World
U. S. S. R., Early Russian Icons
USSR vs. U. S. A.   (USSR versus U. S. A.)
Utopias and Education
Vampire Cookbook

Vancouver's Discovery of Puget Sound
Van Dean Manual
Van Goor's Concise Indonesian Dictionary
Van Nostrand Atlas of the World
Volunteers for Peace
Von Richthofen and the Flying Circus
Von Ryan's Express
Vote and Win
Vote: 1832-1928
Vote for Dick
Vote of Censure
A Walk through Britain
Webster's biographical dictionary
Who am I?
Who was who...
Wholesale and retail trade...
Who'll mind Henry?
Wholly Communion
Whom God Chooses
Whooping Crane
Whoop-up Country
Who's a pest
Who's afraid?
Who's Who
Who's Who in America
Who's who in history
Who's Who in Space
Who's Who of American Women
Whose Eye Am I
Whose world
Works
World list of scientific periodicals
The Writer's handbook
Zenith of European Power
Zero Defects
Zero Is Something
Zero to Zillions
Zero Zero Seven SEE 00 Seven
Zero-Level Additional mathematics
Zoology made simple

Appendix II

Change Over to a Three-Way Divided Card Catalog

Tradition is somewhat like apple pie: too little and we feel the need for more, too much and we soon have another need. The traditional library dictionary card catalog has become a giant apple pie becoming increasingly indigestible. For this reason many librarians have considered dividing their card catalog into author, title, and subject sections. However, the change to a three-way divided card catalog is usually viewed to be a task consuming an undue amount of time. Nevertheless, the change over from a traditional dictionary card catalog to a three-way division need not be burdensome. The change can be made quickly with a minimum of professional supervision.

Certain questions must be asked and decisions made before beginning the change:

1. When is the best time to make a change?
2. How many staff members are needed?
3. How much time will be involved in this change?
4. Which cards go into the author, title, and subject sections?
5. What are the logical steps to initiate this change as rapidly as possible?

Ways and means of aiding in decision-making will be discussed in more detail below. The size of the collection, the staff available, the time involved, and so forth are all interrelated, and they will be dealt with separately for discussion purposes and emphasis.

WHEN?

As soon as possible. Whatever time is lost in making the change will soon be gained in speed of filing and in user appreciation. The work actually falls into five general stages: (1) separating the cards within each drawer in the catalog; (2) removing cards from each drawer; (3) estimating the number of drawers needed for each of the three sections; (4) replacing cards into the card catalog; and (5) re-lettering drawers.

The actual dividing need not be done at one time. Each drawer can be divided into three sections within the drawer itself. All that is needed is a divider clearly indicating the sections within

the drawer: author, title, and subject. Temporarily there will
be three alphabetical groupings within each drawer until all
drawers have been divided in this manner. The card catalog
thus remains as useful as before throughout the sorting process. This makes possible a gradual changeover, particularly
useful for the large library collection, however, by using the
maximum help, the entire change may be made in a few days.

HOW LARGE A STAFF IS NEEDED?

Almost any person having average intelligence and the
ability to ask questions is capable of assisting in this changeover. Both students and other nonprofessional help will need
some instruction. The advantage in having the entire library
professional staff participate in some manner in the instructional program is to bridge the gap between the old and the new
card catalog arrangements. The number of staff needed largely
depends on the decision of whether to make a gradual or an
immediate change.

A Gradual Change:

Assuming that a card catalog drawer is full (about 1,000
cards) one person can divide about six drawers (minimum)
per day into author, title, and subject sections. This means
that one person could separate cards in 120 drawers in
less than a month, four persons could do it in less than a
week. Students could be hired just for the sorting process.
The professional person would then be available for the
occasional question or for making the actual division of
particularly difficult sections of the catalog. It is suggested that no less than two individuals be assigned to the
dividing of cards within drawers even in the smallest
libraries.

Even in a gradual change there comes the time when all
drawers are finished and a "crash" program must be imple-
mented to make the final change. When the crash program
takes place, the choice of those used to supervise and
carry out decisions is most crucial. The number of staff
required is not great, but the precision with which the
changing of cards from drawer to drawer is of the ut-
most importance. The change itself will be discussed in
detail later.

An Immediate Change:

If an immediate change is desired, the maximum number of staff help is a must. It may be necessary to

temporarily close off the card catalog area if several of the
staff are helping in the card separation. Much will depend
on the time of year - choose a time when there is less use
of the library. The proper timing may prevent a need to
close off use of the card catalog. Libraries with a book
collection of over 250,000 volumes will find it too imprac-
tical to make an immediate change without completely
closing off use of the card catalog for several days.

HOW MUCH TIME?

It is possible to estimate the length of time for a change
using the following formula:

> One full catalog drawer (1,000 cards)
> Working day - 6 hours (actual time spent in dividing
>   drawers, minus breaks, etc.)
> One catalog drawer divided each hour (possibly as
>   high as three per hour)
> Hours per day x Persons working = Drawers divided
>   6   x   10   = 60 divided per day

However, in a large library collection more drawers in
the catalog will already consist of all subject cards. This will
greatly increase the number of drawers divided in an hour and
decrease the total time involved in large collection changes.
Approximately one day to a week's time must be planned after
all drawers are divided to make the complete change. If all
cards have been kept in their original order, no need will be
necessary for revision at this time. Later the separate
sections can be revised according to the previous filing rules.
The card catalog can remain in full use at the time of revision.

WHICH CARDS INTO WHICH SECTION?

Certain problems will arise for the professional, and
choices must be made in order to instruct the other staff
members. Librarians may have to change some of their
traditional thinking, but users will find these changes nor-
mal and compatible with their thinking as they approach
the card catalog.

The question will come up, "Do we make title cards for
all books?" We suggest that every book have a title card
including those shown in the examples below. Although there
is really no need to repeat the author's name on the top line,
there is an advantage for the user - speed in locating the
desired book.

PS
3525
A27
A17
1962

Collected poems (MacLeish, Archibald)

MacLeish, Archibald, 1892–
  Collected poems. Boston, Houghton Mifflin ₍°1962₎
  417 p. 21 cm.

E
322
A3

Diary and autobiography . . . (Adams, John)

Adams, John, *Pres. U. S.,* 1735–1826.
  Diary and autobiography. L. H. Butterfield, editor,
Leonard C. Faber and Wendell D. Garrett, assistant editors.
Cambridge, Belknap Press of Harvard University Press,
1961-

  4 v. illus., ports., maps, facsims. 26 cm. (*His* Papers. Series ɪ:
Diaries)

DC
121.7
L6

An introduction to seventeenth century
        France

Lough, John.
  An introduction to seventeenth century France. New York,
D. McKay 1966

  xxiii, 296 p. illus., ports., facsims.   , maps.

  Bibliography : p. 285–291.

PN
1031
D73

Poetry . . . (Drew, Elizabeth A.)

Drew, Elizabeth A   1887–
  Poetry: a modern guide to its understanding and enjoy-
ment. New York, W. W. Norton ₍1959₎
  287 p. 21 cm.

PN
511
.E443
1960

Selected essays . . . (Eliot, T.S.)

Eliot, Thomas Stearns, 1888–
  Selected essays. New ed. New York, Harcourt, Brace
₍1960₎

  xiv, 460 p. 22 cm.

  First ed. (1932) published under title : Selected essays, 1917–1932.

  cl   ALANAR   9/67   6.50

  1. Literature—Addresses, essays, lectures. 2. Criticism.

  PN511.E443 1960   814.52   50—10103

  Library of Congress   ₍60f²₎

Other examples will follow under the specific headings of author, title, and subject. These examples will be sufficient for most libraries. A more extensive list of examples may prove useful and be duplicated for instructional purposes. Something similar to the following must be included in the instructions given to each person helping before any dividing takes place.

Authors:

The author(s) is the one responsible for preparation of a book's content. All of these cards in each drawer are to be brought together into one section. An author may include any of the following:

1. Personal names: authors, joint authors, editors, joint editors, illustrators, compilers, pseudonyms, and translators (no biography or criticism).
2. Names of associations, organizations, firms, societies, etc.
3. Names of places: countries, states, cities, names of governments and their agencies, etc.
4. Institutions: colleges and universities, schools, museums, and other places of learning.
5. Churches and various religious organizations.
6. Series:(It is often difficult to distinguish between author series card and a title series card.)
7. Periodical publisher(This is frequently not found for such as Look or Life)

Please note that this does not mean that all "main entry" cards are considered as author entries in a divided catalog. Examples will be given under Titles. See examples of cards which should be included in the author section of the card catalog.

LA
229
A77

American Council on Education.
The college and the student; an assessment of relation-
ships and responsibilities in undergraduate education by
administrators, faculty members, and public officials.   Editors: Lawrence E. Dennis & Joseph F. Kauffman.   Washington ₁1966₁

DA
428.1   **Ashley, Maurice Percy,** *comp.*
A77   Cromwell, edited by Maurice Ashley.   Englewood Cliffs,
        N. J., Prentice-Hall ₁1969₁

            x, 177 p.   22 cm.   (Great lives observed)   4.95

QH
324
B3   **Baldwin, Ernest.**
1964   An introduction to comparative biochemistry, with a fore-
        word by Sir Frederick Gowland Hopkins.   **4th ed.,** Cam-
        bridge ₁Eng.₁ University Press, **1964.,**

L   Birnbaum, Max, joint author
901   **Cass, James.**
C33   Comparative guide to American colleges, for students,
1965   parents, and counselors, by James Cass and Max Birnbaum.
        New and enl. ed.   New York, Harper & Row ₁1965₁

            xxxiv, 725 p.   24 cm.

Z   Bowker (R. R.) Company, firm, publishers,
1215   New York.
P97   The Publishers' trade list annual.   (Card 2)
                v.   28 cm.   annual.
              Editors: 1948–52, B. A. Uhlendorf.—1953–   H. B. Anstaett.
                            Z1215.P972

QD   Case Institute of Technology, Cleveland.
42
B282   **Barrow, Gordon M**
              Programmed supplements for general chemistry ₁by₁ Gor-
        don M. Barrow ₁and others₁   Case Institute of Technology.
        New York, W. A. Benjamin, 1963–

                v.   diagrs   24 cm.

              1. Chemistry — Programmed instruction.   I. Case Institute of
        Technology, Cleveland.   II. Title.

            QD42.B282   540.7   63–19980

Chandler, Alfred Dupont, *ed.*
The railroads, the Nation's first big business; sources and readings. Compiled and edited by Alfred D. Chandler, Jr. New York, Harcourt, Brace & World [1965]

ix, 213 p. map. 23 cm. (The Forces in American economic growth series)

Bibliography: p. 213. Bibliographical footnotes.

Chicago. University. Law School
The **Supreme Court** review. 1960–
Chicago, University of Chicago Press.

v. 24 cm. annual.

At head of title, 1960–   law school, University of Chicago.
Editor: 1960–   P. B. Kurland.

Council of State Governments
The **Book** of the States. v. 1–   1935–
Chicago, Council of State Governments.

v. illus., ports. 26 cm. biennial.

Dowdey, Clifford, 1904–
The land they fought for; the story of the South as the Confederacy, 1832–1865. [1st ed.] Garden City, N. Y., Doubleday 1955.

viii, 438 p. map (on lining papers) 24 cm. (Mainstream of America series)

Bibliography: p. [416]–426.

Eulau, Heinz, 1915–   *ed.*
Political behavior in America; new directions. New York, Random House [1966]

viii, 532 p. illus. 21 cm.

Includes bibliographical references.

Goodspeed, Edgar Johnson, 1871–   tr.
Bible. *English. 1939. Smith-Goodspeed.*
The complete Bible, an American translation; the Old Testament translated by J. M. Powis Smith and a group of scholars; the Apocrypha and the New Testament translated by Edgar J. Goodspeed. Chicago, Ill., the University of Chicago press [C1948]

xvi p., 1 l., 883, iv, 202, iv, 246, [1] p. 20 cm.

The Old Testament, an American translation by A. R. Gordon, T. J. Meek, J. M. P. Smith, Leroy Waterman; edited by J. M. P. Smith; revised by T. J. Meek. *cf.* p. [xi]

I. Smith, John Merlin Powis, 1866–1932, ed. II. Goodspeed, Edgar Johnson, 1871–   tr. III. Meek, Theophile James, 1881–   ed. IV. Title.

BS195.S6   1939   220.52   39—28964

Library of Congress   [6112]

Nobelstiftelsen, *Stockholm.*
    Nobel, the man and his prizes, by H. Schück [and others.
2d rev. and enl. ed.] Amsterdam, New York, Elsevier Pub.
Co.; [sole distributor for the U. S.: American Elsevier Pub.

Rand McNally and Company.
    Rand McNally atlas of world history, edited by R. R.
Palmer; contributing editors: Knight Biggerstaff [and
others] Chicago [1965]

Stanford University. Institute for the
Study of Human Problems .

Katz, Joseph, 1920–
    No time for youth; growth and constraint in college stu-
dents [by] Joseph Katz & associates: Harold A. Korn [and
others. 1st ed.] San Francisco, Jossey-Bass, 1968.

Tarkington, Booth, 1869–1946.
    Alice Adams. New York, Grosset & Dunlap [1961, °1921]
        434 p. 20 cm.

Twain, Mark, pseud.

SEE

Clemens, Samuel Langhorne, 1835-1910

U. S. *Bureau of the Census.*
    Historical statistics of the United States, colonial times to
1957; a Statistical abstract supplement. Prepared with the
cooperation of the Social Science Research Council. [Wash-
ington, For sale by the Superintendent of Documents, U. S.
Govt. Print. Off., 1960]

U. S. *Post Office Dept.*
    National Zip code directory. Washington [Bureau of
Operations; for sale by the Superintendent of Documents,
U. S. Govt. Print. Off.] 1966.
        xiii, 1772 p. 28 cm. (*Its* POD publication 65)

    1. Zip code—U. S.   I. Title.   II. Title: Zip code directory.
(Series)

    HE6311.A3 no. 65 1966   383.4902573   66–60919

Titles:
    Title entries include any of the following;
1. The title of a book as listed on the card under the author's name
2. Entries without authors
3. The Bible and other sacred books
4. Anonymous classics
5. Title series
6. Names of periodicals and indexes

BS
195
S6
1939

Bible. *English. 1939. Smith-Goodspeed.*
    The complete Bible, an American translation; the Old Testament translated by J. M. Powis Smith and a group of scholars; the Apocrypha and the New Testament translated by Edgar J. Goodspeed. Chicago, Ill., the University of Chicago press [ᶜ1948]

Z
5112
B56

Biennial review of anthropology. v. 1–
    1959–
    Stanford, Calif., Stanford University Press.

AE
5
C443
1967

Chambers's encyclopaedia. New rev. ed. Oxford, New York, Pergamon Press [1967, ᶜ1966]
    15 v. illus. (part col.) 28 cm.

QP
511
C47

The **Chemistry** of life; eight lectures on the history of biochemistry, by Robert Hill [and others]. Edited with and introduction by Joseph Needham. Cambridge [Eng.] University Press, 1970.

QH
366
S58

The meaning of evolution.
Simpson, George Gaylord, 1902–
    The meaning of evolution, a study of the history of life and of its significance for man. New Haven, Yale University Press, 1949.

PE
1628
S586
1966

Funk & Wagnalls Standard college dictionary. New York, Funk & Wagnalls [1966]

PS
169
F7
H3

The frontier in American literature
Hazard, Lucy Lockwood, 1890–
    The frontier in American literature, by Lucy Lockwood Hazard. New York, Thomas Y. Crowell company [ᶜ1927]

E
173
C55
v.56

The Chronicles of America series, V. 56
Nevins, Allan, 1890–
    The New Deal and world affairs; a chronicle of international affairs, 1933–1945. New Haven, Yale University Press, 1950.
        ix, 332 p. ports. 21 cm. (The Chronicles of America series, v. 56)
        "Bibliographical notes": p. 315–321.

        1. U. S.—For. rel.—1933–1945. 2. World politics. I. Title.
    (Series)
                       Full name: Joseph Allan Nevins.

    E173.C55   vol. 56   327.73   50—8828
    —— —— Copy 2.   E744.N487

    Library of Congress   [58f²]

PR
1221
079

The **Oxford** book of nineteenth-century English verse, chosen
by John Hayward. Oxford, Clarendon Press, 1964.

xxxv, 969 p. 20 cm.

CB
59
M3

The rise of the West

McNeill, William Hardy, 1917–
  The rise of the West; a history of the human community.
Drawings by Béla Petheö. Chicago, University of Chicago
Press ₁1963₁

829 p. illus. 25 cm.

REF
BR
95
S43
1964

Schaff-Herzog encyclopedia.
  The new Schaff-Herzog encyclopedia of religious knowledge, embracing Biblical, historical, doctrinal, and practical
theology, and Biblical, theological, and ecclesiastical biogra-

QH
366
S58

The Terry lectures, Yale University

Simpson, George Gaylord, 1902–
  The meaning of evolution, a study of the history of life
and of its significance for man. **New Haven, Yale University Press, 1949.**

xv, 364 p. illus. 21 cm. (The Terry lectures)

REF
BR
95
S43
1964

Twentieth century encyclopedia of
  religious knowledge.

Schaff-Herzog encyclopedia.
  The new Schaff-Herzog encyclopedia of religious knowledge, embracing Biblical, historical, doctrinal, and practical
theology, and Biblical, theological, and ecclesiastical biography from the earliest times to the present day; based on the

See
Film
Library

Use of pipette (*Motion picture*) Ealing Corp., 1967. Made
by Ealing Corp. with Richard M. Whitney.
  4 min. si. color. 8 mm. (Chemistry laboratory technique series)
  A loop film mounted in cartridge.
  16 mm. and super 8 mm. versions also issued.
  With film notes on cartridge case.
  Summary: Demonstrates the use of three types of pipettes: transfer, measuring, and bulb. Shows the uses of a 5 ml transfer pipette
in conjunction with a 500 ml volumetric flask to produce a 0.01 M
solution of a chemical by diluting a 1 M source, the measuring pipette
to dispense 4 ml of a liquid into one test tube and 6 ml into another,
and the bulb pipette to extract and transfer a known volume of a
radioactive liquid.
  1. Pipettes.   i. Ealing Corporation, Cambridge, Mass.   Series:
Chemistry laboratory technique series (Motion picture)

Fi A 66–1793

Ealing Corporation
for Library of Congress   ₁3₁

Subjects:

Most libraries either type subject headings in all capitals or in red. Subject headings should therefore be obvious. Subject cards include those about persons: biography and criticism.

HF
5341
B4
1963

COMMERCE—HISTORY

Beard, Miriam, 1901–
 A history of business: from the monopolists to the organization man. ₍Ann Arbor₎ The University of Michigan Press ₍ᶜ1963₎

  292 p. (Ann Arbor paperbacks, AA76. A History of business, v. 2)

  Bibliography: p. 285-287.

MT
90
T6
E8

MUSIC—ANALYTICAL GUIDES

Tovey, *Sir* **Donald Francis,** 1875–1940.
 Essays in musical analysis, by Donald Francis Tovey ... London, Oxford university press, H. Milford ₍1936–66₎

 6 v. illus. (music)

  CONTENTS. — I. Symphonies. — II. Symphonies (II), Variations and orchestral polyphony. — III. Concertos. — IV. Illustrative music. — V. Vocal music.—VI. Miscellaneous notes, glossary and index.

MT
95
K52
1963

OPERAS - STORIES, PLOTS, ETC.

Kobbé, Gustav, 1857–1918.
 Complete opera book. Edited and rev. by the Earl of Harewood. London, New York, Putnam ₍1963₎

 xvi, 1262 p. 40 plates (incl. ports) music. 22 cm.

E
173
C55
V23

SPAIN—COLONIES—NORTH AMERICA

Bolton, Herbert Eugene, 1870–
 The Spanish borderlands: a chronicle of old Florida and the Southwest, by Herbert E. Bolton. New Haven, Yale university press; ₍etc., etc.₎ ₍1921₎

  xiv, 320 p. front. (port.) plates, fold. map. 21 cm. (*Half-title:* The chronicles of America series, Allen Johnson, editor ... v. 23)
  "Textbook edition."
  "Bibliographical note": p. 297-303.

U. S. - HISTORY ATLASES

  SEE.

 U. S. - HISTORICAL GEOGRAPHY - MAPS

STEPS NEEDED TO INITIATE THE CHANGE
1. Assignment of one professional to act as coordinator. In large libraries more than one coordinator may be needed.
2. Agreement among staff. Every decision should be in writing and well illustrated. Duplicate these instructions. Good illustrations and examples are about the only means of avoiding errors and misunderstanding.
3. Instruction. Everyone on the library staff must be indoctrinated in the change. Along with good explanations and illustrations a very effective means of training is the use of a practice file. This file is arranged in a typical dictionary card catalog manner. It is composed of about 100 cards with "difficult" headings. Require each staff member to rearrange the practice drawer into three divisions until they do it correctly. The practice cards should be numbered consecutively on the back side of card both according to the dictionary alphabetical arrangement and the divided arrangement. This will facilitate replacing cards into a dictionary arrangement and also help in checking the divided arrangement. Most problems will come up at this time. Posters showing users what is taking place with the card catalog will be appreciated.
4. Training. Although the entire staff needs to read and use the practice file, additional training may need to be given and new help brought in specifically for the change. A thorough explanation of a catalog card format is important. Use such an illustration as follows:

E
77
W779
1966

Wissler, Clark, 1870–1947.
     Indians of the United States. Rev. ed. Revisions pre-
pared by Lucy Wales Kluckhohn. Garden City, N. Y.,
Doubleday, 1966.

     336 p.   map, plates, ports.   24 cm.

     Bibliography : p. ₁305₁–319.

E   INDIANS OF NORTH AMERICA--HISTORY
77   **Wissler, Clark,** 1870–1947.
W779   Indians of the United States. Rev. ed. Revisions pre-
1966   pared by Lucy Wales Kluckhohn. Garden City, N. Y.,
         Doubleday, 1966.

              336 p.   map, plates, ports.   24 cm.

              Bibliography : p. ₁305₁–319.

         INDIANS OF NORTH AMERICA—SOCIAL
E   LIFE AND CUSTOMS
77   **Wissler, Clark,** 1870–1947.
W779   Indians of the United States. Rev. ed. Revisions pre-
1966   pared by Lucy Wales Kluckhohn. Garden City, N. Y.,
         Doubleday, 1966.

              336 p.   map, plates, ports.   24 cm.

              Bibliography : p. ₁305₁–319.

E   Kluckhohn, Lucy Wales, ed.
77   **Wissler, Clark,** 1870–1947.
W779   Indians of the United States. Rev. ed. Revisions pre-
1966   pared by Lucy Wales Kluckhohn. Garden City, N. Y.,
         Doubleday, 1966.

              336 p.   map, plates, ports.   24 cm.

              Bibliography : p. ₁305₁–319.

         Indians of the United States.
E
77   **Wissler, Clark,** 1870–1947.
W779   Indians of the United States. Rev. ed. Revisions pre-
1966   pared by Lucy Wales Kluckhohn. Garden City, N. Y.,
         Doubleday, 1966.

              336 p.   map, plates, ports.   24 cm.

              Bibliography : p. ₁305₁–319.

         1. Indians of North America—Hist.   2. Indians of North Amer-
     ica—Soc. life & cust.   I. Kluckhohn, Lucy Wales, ed.   II. Title.

     E77.W779   1966   970.43   66–12215

     Library of Congress   ₁5₁

5. Division of catalog drawer. The following actions in dividing
a catalog drawer are required: (Only two divider cards are
needed for each drawer, a TITLE and SUBJECT divider.
The author card divider is not needed if author cards are
kept in the front of each drawer.)
   (a) Place both Title and Subject dividers behind all cards in
the drawer.
   (b) As you go through the cards, one at a time, keep all
author cards in the front of drawer. Remove title or
subject cards and place behind the correct divider. All
subsequent cards are placed at the rear of their section.
This will keep all cards in their original alphabetical order.
   (c) When the drawer is finished it will look something like
this:

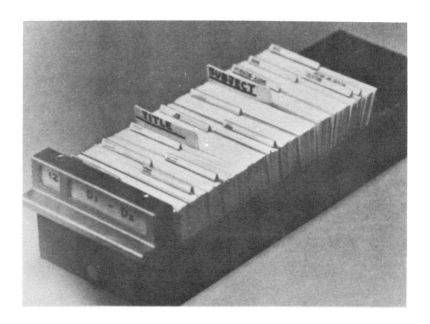

6. Separation of sections. When all drawers are divided and it is time to make the change into the three separated sections, place rubber bands around cards in each drawer, keeping author, title, and subject sections separate.
7. Removal of cards from the drawers.
   (a) Do not use the card catalog while this takes place.
   (b) Have one person responsible for withdrawing each section. The fewer persons involved at this point, the better.
   (c) Select a large room or hallway and line up the cards in alphabetical order on the floor (or tables). In large collections, use a separate room for each division of the catalog.
   (d) Estimate total number of inches in each section.
   (e) Estimate the number of inches to allow in each drawer. Divide the inches to be allowed in each drawer into the total number of inches of that division to determine the drawers needed for that section. Cards may be divided at this point into, e.g., eight inch groups and held in place with rubber bands. At this point don't bother making decisions as to the best point to divide cards between drawers. The important part now is to replace the cards into the drawers as soon as possible.
8. Location. Relocate catalog sections and cabinets. Allow the most user room for the subject section as it tends to be used more frequently.
9. Replacing cards. Replace cards in catalog drawers according to your groupings in 7e. If handled in this fashion the cards will be replaced in the card catalog very rapidly.
10. Marking drawers. Re-mark each drawer - use temporary guides at first. A careful dividing of cards between each drawer may take time and thought.
11. Checking. Check the author, title, and subject sections by the filing rules covered in this book.

ADDITIONAL SUGGESTIONS:
   1. Separate Biography and Criticism cards into a completely separate card catalog section.
   2. Make subject guides for all subjects (only practical in large collections) and file all cards for this subject behind the guide without retyping heading on each card.

3. If number two above is followed, file cards behind each
   heading guide card chronologically by publication date,
   the latest date being first. This makes for easy filing
   and aids the user to quickly find the most recent material.

Appendix III

Examination

The reader can test his comprehension of the previous rule by answering the following questions. Answers for each questio along with the specific rule involved, are given follwing the questions.

1. Arrange this list alphabetically word-by-word and then let ter-by-letter
   Washers
   Wash tubs
   Washing
   Washer solvent
   Wash basins
2. Spell out the following numbers as spoken in the language of the title as you would file them.
   F-86 Sabre
   D-99 Reader
   6 1/2 West Haven Street
   1001 Magic Tricks
   First 150 years
3. Spell out the following dates as spoken in the language of the title as you would file them.
   The War of 1919
   1914 Diary
   France: 1814-1919
   History, 1942 Style
   The Year 2000
4. Give various examples of how "007" might be spelled out i the language of the title.
5. Make the necessary cross reference cards for this list.
   Title Cards
   Downtown U.S.A.
   Dr. Albert Schweitzer, Medical Missionary
   Dr. Spock Talks to Mothers
   Dracula
   The U.S. at War

6. Arrange these names in proper alphabetical order.
>   De Leiris
>   Delgado
>   De La Mare
>   Del Bagno
>   Delbo
>   De La Roche
>   Del Bo, Dino

7. Alphabetize the following subject headings:
>   EDUCATION-BIBLIOGRAPHY
>   EDUCATION-HISTORY
>   EDUCATION-SOUTH AFRICA
>   EDUCATION, ELEMENTARY
>   EDUCATION, HIGHER
>   EDUCATION, SECONDARY
>   EDUCATION AND STATE

8. Which list is correct?

"A"	"B"
Henry, Carl	Henry, Carl, 1891-1847
Henry, Carl, 1891-1847	Henry, Carl
Henry, Charles	Henry, Charles

9. Are the following questions true or false?
   (a) All main entry cards are filed in the author section of the card catalog.
   (b) All numerals (dates and numbers) within a heading are ignored in alphabetizing, except when they are needed to distinguish between two like entries.
   (c) Arrange initials as though they were separate words.
   (d) Arrange initials as though spelled in full.
   (e) Compound names without a hyphen are filed as one word.
   (f) Arrange all names with a prefix as one word.
   (g) Hyphenated words or names are arranged as one word.
   (h) Disregard all signs and symbols in titles.
   (i) Lengthy added headings requiring two or more lines for typing are treated as though it were all one continuous line for alphabetical purposes.

Answers to Questions

1. Word-by-word	Letter-by-letter
Wash basins	Wash basins
Wash tubs	Washers
Washer solvent	Washer solvent
Washers	Washing
Washing	Wash tubs
(Rule I)	

2. F-Eighty-six Sabre
   D-Ninety-nine Reader
   Six and one half West Haven Street
   One Thousand One Magic Tricks
   First One Hundred Fifty Years
        (Rule V, point 1)
3. The War of Nineteen Nineteen
   Nineteen Fourteen Diary
   France: Eighteen Fourteen-Nineteen Nineteen
   History, Nineteen Forty-two Style
   The Year Two Thousand
        (Rule V, point 1)
4. 00 Seven
   Double 0 Seven
   Zero Zero Seven
   Double Zero Seven
        This necessitates making a cross-reference from the
   forms not used to the one used.
        (Rule V, point 1, d)
5. Dr. SEE ALSO Doctor
   Doctor SEE ALSO Dr.
   U.S. SEE ALSO United States
   United States SEE ALSO U.S.
        (Rule IV, point 2; Rule VIII)
6. De La Mare
   De La Roche
   Del Bagno
   Delbo
   Del Bo, Dino
   De Leiris
   Delgado
        (Rule III, point 1, 5)
7. EDUCATION AND STATE
   EDUCATION-BIBLIOGRAPHY
   EDUCATION, ELEMENTARY
   EDUCATION, HIGHER
   EDUCATION-HISTORY
   EDUCATION, SECONDARY
   EDUCATION-SOUTH AFRICA
        (Rule II, point 1)
8. "A"
        (Rule III, point 3, subject point 5)

9. (a) False   (Rule VII, point 1)
    (b) True   (Rule V, point 2, b)
    (c) False   (Rule IV, point 3)
    (d) False   (Rule IV, point 2)
    (e) False   (Rule III, point 2)
    (f) True   (Rule III, point 1)
    (g) True   (Rule II, point 7)
    (h) False   (Rule II, point 3)
    (i) True   (Rule I, d)

Index